The Church in
South Africa

CHURCH HISTORY OUTLINES
EDITED BY V. H. H. GREEN, D.D.

The Church in South Africa

PETER HINCHLIFF

Professor of Ecclesiastical History in Rhodes University
Grahamstown, South Africa

LONDON
S · P · C · K
for the Church Historical Society
1968

First published in 1968
by S.P.C.K.
Holy Trinity Church
Marylebone Road
London N.W.1

Made and printed in Great Britain by
William Clowes and Sons, Limited
London and Beccles

SBN 281 02277 1

For
Nicholas, Susan, Richard, and Jeremy,
when they are a bit older

Contents

MAP   viii

FOREWORD   ix

PREFACE   xi

1   The Cape and the Dutch East India Company   1

2   "Cuius Regio Eius Religio": The Moravian Mission   8

3   The Dutch Reformed and Anglican Establishments   13

4   Vanderkemp and Philip of the London Missionary
    Society   22

5   1820 and the beginnings of Methodism   29

6   The Dutch Reformed Church and the Great Trek   36

7   Frontier and Mission   43

8   Livingstone and Exploration   52

9   The Origins of the "Hervormde" and
    "Gereformeerde" Churches   58

10 Bishop Colenso   65

11 Missionary Conflict and Growth in the North   72

12 Andrew Murray and the Struggle between Liberals
    and Conservatives in the Dutch Reformed Church   79

13 Scottish Missions and Education   85

14 Ethiopianism: Christianity and Politics   90

15 Some Recent Developments   98

BIBLIOGRAPHY   108

INDEX   113

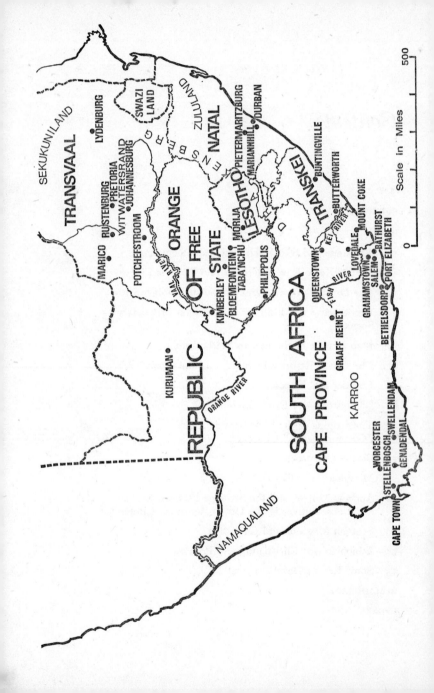

Foreword

"The first of human concerns", Lord Acton observed in his inaugural lecture at Cambridge in 1895, "is religion, and it is the salient feature of the modern centuries." Nor can there be much doubt that even in an age more secular than that in which Lord Acton lived the history of the Christian Church continues to be a matter of perennial fascination. For the layman it serves to illuminate the whole field of human activity, being a necessary adjunct to the true interpretation of history. For the committed Christian, aware that his faith is founded on a historical religion, the history of the Church may offer an interpretation of the meaning of the process of human history and even of the purpose of life itself. In the past the history of the Church was too often the instrument of propagandists and polemists. With the growth of a more scientific attitude to history our understanding of the Church has been enriched by specialized works of research and learned monographs, so much so that the intelligent reader may often find himself baffled by the extent of the published material which confronts him. There seems indeed a need to present the findings of modern research in popular fashion and to relate them to topics of Church history which are of continuous interest and importance. It is perhaps equally important to find a popular medium by which the interested reader can find information about topics which are not ordinarily available to him in the existing history books. This series of booklets is intended to fulfil one or other of these objects, to represent studies of significant movements and to open up new subjects. I very much hope that in this way more people will be drawn to an understanding of Church history and become aware of its significance. For Church history is not simply a matter of the past alone. Anyone who is concerned with the future development of the Church, its evangelistic purpose, the problem of reunion, its attitude to secular movements and so forth, may well find that the history of the past bears powerfully on the present and may constitute a signpost to the future.

V. H. H. GREEN

Preface

Obviously a book of this size cannot make any original contribution to knowledge. It is chiefly the result of a putting together of material taken from the work of others. But there is no single account of the history of Christianity in South Africa. There are denominational histories, missionary histories, biographies, and some specialized works (mostly unpublished). I have tried to put them together to make one coherent story.

The result must be regarded as a tentative and preliminary account. A vast amount of material needs to be examined still. But perhaps if there is some sort of framework it will be easier to see where further research is most urgently needed. As this research is done my present conclusions will certainly need a good deal of revision.

Inevitably there will be those who will feel that I have omitted many vital episodes from the story. Some of the most active missionary bodies, for instance, have been hardly mentioned. Events which were of great significance for particular denominations may have been omitted altogether. But it was impossible to deal adequately with everything. One has to make one's selection and stick to it.

I have to acknowledge my dependence on sources far too numerous to name individually. Some of them are listed in the bibliography, which is a selective one. I have, on the whole, tried to restrict it to books, but for the sake of the student who may have both the need and the opportunity to pursue the subject further I have included a few unpublished theses. Scholars of the Afrikaans Churches have published a good deal, but for some other episodes or topics I have dealt with the only available source was unpublished.

I am grateful for the help and advice I have received from a great many people, including the Reverend Dr D. G. L. Cragg, Dr T. R. H. Davenport, the Reverend Professor L. A. Hewson, and the Reverend M. Nuttall. I am also extremely grateful to Mrs M. Hoyle for typing the manuscript.

PETER HINCHLIFF

1. The Cape and the Dutch East India Company

Other Western European explorers visited or circumnavigated the southern tip of Africa, but it was the Dutch, in the middle of the seventeenth century, who were the first white men to settle within the boundaries of modern South Africa and it was they who first brought Christianity. They came, not as missionaries, but as the agents of commerce—but they brought their religion with them and Christian history in South Africa must begin with them.

Before the Dutch came the country was already inhabited by a mixture of races. In the west, where the Dutch landed, there were Bushmen who have been described as relics of the Stone Age. Contact between these people and the white men was not to play a large part in the later history of South Africa. They were nomads and hunters. They died out or were exterminated or withdrew to the desert regions of the interior. They never became a part of the settled structure of the country.

Far more prominent in the history of the Dutch settlement were the Hottentots. Clans of these people were to be found right across the southern part of the continent from South-West Africa to Natal. They were more "civilized" than the Bushman, herders of cattle rather than hunters. Like the Bushmen, they tended in time to disappear. They were decimated by disease. They intermarried with the half-caste population and with other races. But they play a considerable part in the story of the early expansion of the settlement.

In the eastern part of the sub-continent were the African people, the Bantu or Nguni. These people were darker, taller, more "civilized" still than either the Bushmen or the Hottentots. They came down into what is now South Africa from the north.

This much, at least, seems to be accepted. It used to be said that their arrival in the eastern Cape took place at very much the same time as the arrival of the Dutch in the west. But it is possible that it happened much earlier. "The Portuguese records show that from 1554 there were people 'very black in colour' south of the Mtata river [i.e. in the modern Transkei], and a little further north 'the country was thickly populated and provided with cattle'. From 1593 there is evidence that the people south of the Mtata spoke an Nguni language, and from 1686 we can place the various Xhosa-speaking tribes known today; they occupied the country from the Buffalo (East London) northwards."[1]

When the Dutch landed in 1652 the position was that Bushmen and Hottentots were to be found in small groups right across what was to become the Cape Colony, and in the west these were the only inhabitants. In the east there were the African tribes and their general tendency was to move westward. It must not be thought that these three peoples lived in separate and exclusive areas. All three might occupy the same area and might indeed be living side by side. We have no means of knowing the size of the population, but it would seem likely that, apart from the eastern districts of the present Cape Province, it was not very dense.

The party from Holland made little difference to the over-all population of the country. The young commander of the party, van Riebeeck, came with about eighty men in three ships. He was instructed to build a fort large enough to hold his followers. And it was drummed into him that his job was to ensure that fresh provisions were available for passing ships. This was not a colony. It was hardly even a settlement. It is perhaps best thought of as a station of the Dutch East India Company, comparable in a sense with modern weather stations established on remote and not very habitable islands. It had, that is to say, a utilitarian purpose within the framework of the general life of the Company. It was never intended that it should become the permanent home of these expatriate Dutchmen.

The Company was already past its heyday. Begun as a state-sponsored combine of hitherto rival trading firms, the Company

[1] M. Wilson, "The Early History of the Transkei and Ciskei", *African Studies*, Vol. 18, No. 4, p. 178.

had become a vast colonial power. Although the state claimed sovereignty over its possessions, the real authority lay in the hands of the famous Council of Seventeen, the directorate of the Company. A governor-general in Batavia was the highest authority abroad. Under him were governors in the other colonies. But colonies were, in a sense, irrelevant—or relevant only in so far as they were a necessary part of the real concern of the Company, trade and commerce. It was no part of the Company's job to colonize or to evangelize the Cape.

Van Riebeeck seems himself to have believed that the settlement would be viable only if this policy were reversed and if colonists were allowed to make their homes in the countryside about his fort. Seven years after his arrival the Company grudgingly allowed nine men to settle as colonists not directly in the employ of the Company itself. But the policy remained in principle unchanged. The Company wanted fresh water, meat, and vegetables from the Cape. It did not want the trouble and expense that a colony inevitably causes for its masters.

Nor were the authorities much concerned with the religious needs of the Cape. It is true that very early in its history the Company had sent an official to the East with instructions to correct, instruct, and baptize the heathen. It is also true that, from the beginning of the seventeenth century, missionaries were sent to the East Indies. In this the Dutch East India Company was very different from its English rival, which feared that missionaries would be a menace to the best commercial interests. But there were, nevertheless, many reasons why the Dutch Company was slow to begin missionary work at the Cape.

It was, in part, a result of the general unwillingness to convert the Cape into a permanent colony. Even the Company's servants were not well provided for in matters of religion. From 1652 to 1665 there was no permanent minister at the Cape. Occasionally some clergyman off a passing ship might take a service while he was with the settlers. A so-called "sick-comforter" had normally to provide such spiritual ministrations as he was allowed to perform. These were not very many. He could not perform burials, nor administer the sacraments, nor preach (except by reading the sermons of some ordained minister). So long as the Dutch themselves were so poorly provided for, there could be no hope that the Christian religion would be taken to the heathen.

Moreover the Church in Holland had very firm beliefs about baptizing the heathen. Calvin had maintained that it was wrong for a layman to baptize (even in an emergency), not only because this was a usurpation of a ministerial function, but also because he rejected the idea that baptism was necessary for salvation. He believed that infant baptism was right and proper and that it symbolized in a particularly apt manner the true meaning of the sacrament. But such infant baptism was proper only because the children of Christians are already within the covenant.

So it was the view of the Reformed Church in Holland that infant baptism was a privilege to be given only to the children of Christian parents. At the nineteenth session of the Synod of Dort (1618), the great confessional assembly of the Dutch Reformed Church, it had been declared that the children of heathen were not to be baptized, even if they had been taken into Christian households and would be brought up in the Christian way of life. Quite clearly, then, so long as there was no ordained minister at the Cape, none of the heathen could be baptized and even when a minister was appointed he would have to proceed very carefully and slowly. The baptism of infant or uninstructed heathen was unlawful. The whole weight of Reformed tradition was opposed to any missionary haste.

Moreover, if missions were to be undertaken at the Cape, then the Hottentots provided the obvious field. But inevitably there was a great gulf between the Dutch settlers and the Hottentots. The settlers were products of the commercial class of a nation which was proverbial in the seventeenth century for its business sense. The Hottentots were primitive nomads who placed little value upon the middle-class virtues of property and hard work! The settlers thought they exhibited every possible laziness and vice, only occasionally linked with a certain charm. Perhaps at first, even, the Dutch drew no clear distinction between the Bushmen and the Hottentots. They were all "dull, stupid, lazy, and stinking".

And yet the records suggest that the settlers regarded the real barrier between themselves and the Hottentots to be one of religion. In 1662 a Hottentot, Eva, was baptized and was later married to the assistant surgeon of the settlement. Heathenism not colour was evidently the chief barrier to intermarriage. The first school in the Cape, which was established in the following year, included four slaves and a Hottentot amongst its predominantly Dutch pupils. But Eva's case did not turn out happily and perhaps it was not a popular precedent. Most of the heathen baptized in the period from 1652 to 1700 were, in any case, slaves and not Hottentots. Once baptized they were entitled to be treated as almost the equals of the white settlers, and the profession of Christianity was one of the grounds upon which a slave might seek manumission. Under these circumstances it was, perhaps, only to be expected that the spread of the Christian gospel should not be encouraged enthusiastically. A very great strain was obviously placed on the evangelical zeal of the slave-owner. It is not so often realized that the slaves themselves must have been subjected to a very great temptation to pretend to be converted. At all events such missionary work as was done was done in and through the homes of the settlers and there was never a great deal of it.

Meanwhile the organization of the Dutch Reformed Church at the Cape began to grow. The first minister, Johan van Arckel, came to the Cape in 1665 and a consistory was formed. It was subject to the control of the Amsterdam *classis* or presbytery. Yet the Cape consistory sometimes acted independently. It allowed the baptism of children of slaves if a white person guaranteed that they would be brought up as Christians, in spite of the contrary decision taken at Dort.

The station at the Cape became a settlement, and the settlement a colony. Van Riebeeck's plan to allow some farmers and permanent residents at the Cape was dictated by a desire to reduce the cost of maintaining the station and to strengthen his command by increasing the population and, thereby, the potential "garrison". But official policy continued to favour the other and older view of the purpose of the Cape station. Unrest among the Hottentots also tended to discourage colonization. But towards the end of the seventeenth century the Company changed its policy, believing that colonization was the only means by which the necessary supplies of fresh food and water could be provided and the defence of the Cape maintained without disproportionate cost. Under Simon van der Stel, appointed commander in 1679 and subsequently the first governor, new areas were opened up for settlement. Free burghers were encouraged to take farms and even allowed to participate in local government.

Since this was the seventeenth century the principle that the religion of the government ought to be the religion of the people was still regarded as fundamental to the religious settlement of Europe. The Dutch Church was expected to be the Church of all Dutch territories. Its monopoly was challenged, in the mildest possible way, by the arrival of the Huguenots at the Cape in 1688. Since the Edict of Nantes in 1598 the French Huguenots had enjoyed some degree of toleration. The revocation of the edict (1685) drove them to seek religious liberty outside France. In the Low Countries the Dutch Reformed Church, itself Calvinist in belief, was ready to welcome them. The Dutch East India Company agreed to sponsor a group of about 200 of the Huguenots who were willing to emigrate to the Cape.

Since these emigrants represented about one sixth of the total white population of the colony it was regarded as important to absorb them into the Dutch community. This policy of absorption also had a religious significance. The Company had promised the Huguenots that they would be allowed a French pastor in the Drakenstein area, on the fringes of the colony. Within twelve months the French had applied for permission to become a separate congregation with a consistory of their own. Van der Stel refused this request with some heat and passion—they would be asking next for their own magistrate, governor, and prince.

It is plain that van der Stel was again thinking primarily in political terms, but his reaction shows how closely politics and religion were interwoven in the period. It is true that the Company reversed his decision and gave permission for the establishment of a separate consistory. But the members of the consistory were to be bilingual, political commissioners were to attend its meetings, and all important matters were reserved to the Church authorities in Cape Town. The Company also directed that as soon as it was humanly possible, and the rising generation of Huguenot children had been taught Dutch, the French were to lose their language privileges. When their pastor retired the older people protested that they found it difficult to learn Dutch at their age. They were indeed sent another French-speaking pastor but he was instructed to preach in the official language. Only as a great concession was he permitted to preach in French on alternate Sundays. It was plain that even minor differences in religion would be ruthlessly discouraged.

2. "Cuius Regio Eius Religio" The Moravian Mission

If the seventeenth century was not a period of vigorous evangelistic activity at the Cape, the first quarter of the eighteenth century was even worse. Various factors tended to separate the settlers and the Hottentots and to make casual evangelism difficult. Organized missions did not exist. Pastors were now regularly appointed to serve the white community and were paid by the Company, but there were not enough of them to do the work. By 1750 there were about 5,500 white inhabitants of the colony. To care for their spiritual needs there were three ministers, one at Cape Town, one at Stellenbosch, and one at Drakenstein. The settlers were scattered over a wide area, sometimes two or three days' journey from the nearest church and pastor. Under these circumstances it was useless to hope that the clergy would be able to do anything about missions. It is to their credit that they were conscientious about instructing slaves. More than this they could not do.

In such a desperate situation, desperate measures had to be taken. The administration resolved to build new churches and, if necessary, to impress chaplains from passing ships to serve in the colony. But for missions there were neither the men, the time, nor the money. The great period of prosperity for the Company was already drawing to a close. Moreover the eighteenth century was by and large a somewhat rationalistic age averse to missionary enthusiasm. In the Low Countries, as orthodox Calvinism became more rigid and splintered by faction, the Dutch Church suspected change and determined to preserve its position. As a result more and more people became indifferent. Under these circumstances missionary fervour could not flourish.

The best that can be said of the situation in the Cape in the early eighteenth century is that there were a few individuals who still believed that the Christian gospel must be preached to the heathen who surrounded them. But these were individuals who saw the need for missions, only to have their attempts at action frustrated. Pious colonists adopted as their own the foundling children of callous Hottentot parents and educated them as Christians. Others tried to teach the faith to their slaves. If this was all the light which could be generated in a quarter of a century it was a flickering light indeed.

Into this situation came the first real missionary in South Africa, the Moravian Georg Schmidt. The Moravian *Unitas Fratrum* was a Protestant Society which traced its origins to Jan Hus and the fifteenth-century Utraquist movement in Bohemia. It had recently been injected with new life under the leadership of Nicholas Zinzendorf, a Saxon nobleman, a Lutheran who developed a mystical and pietistic faith. In 1727 he created on his estates at Herrnhut a religious community to which he tried to attract Protestant refugees from all over Europe, including many Moravians. Zinzendorf dominated this community and in 1737 was consecrated by Jablonski, a Moravian bishop. The Herrnhut community became virtually an *ecclesiola*, a little Church, within the Lutheran Church as a whole.

Schmidt, who had gone to Herrnhut in 1725, had undertaken missionary work in Bohemia, suffered imprisonment, and even made some sort of recantation of his faith; in expiation his brethren at Herrnhut sent him on his own on a mission to the Cape Hottentots. He undertook his journey with the approval of the Dutch East India Company and after he had been examined by the authorities of the Dutch Church. A good many people had begun to feel some anxiety because the Cape Hottentots had so little opportunity to hear the Gospel.

On his arrival at Cape Town in July 1737 Schmidt was given a very mixed reception. The governor and his council approved as did many of the local inhabitants who were Lutherans; but the majority, believing that the Hottentots were constitutionally incapable of religious belief, regarded him with puzzled hilarity. The Dutch Reformed ministers were very suspicious of him and were determined that he should not be authorized to baptize. In

September 1737 Schmidt moved out to his proposed mission station, which was in time to become the famous Moravian mission station of Genadendal.

Schmidt settled among the Hottentots and began patiently to try to teach them the rudiments of the Christian faith. He had initial disadvantages which he never overcame; youth, inexperience, a certain rigidity of outlook, and spiritual isolation. He tried but was unable to master the language. Yet he persisted in his endeavour to transmit Christian ideas, establishing classes for children and adults, holding Sunday services and even instituting a fellowship meal modelled on the *agape* supper which accompanied the Eucharist in the primitive Church. His real difficulties, however, started when he began to baptize his converts. Although he was authorized to do so by Zinzendorf, the Dutch Reformed ministers thought the procedure irregular, and he was forbidden to perform the sacraments until the presbytery at Amsterdam gave permission. In the event Schmidt, frustrated and disappointed, returned to Europe in 1744 before the unfavourable verdict of the pastors of Amsterdam reached the Cape.

After this, missions in the Cape ceased to exist for nearly fifty years and then, when the Dutch East India Company was almost on its last legs, there came something of a revival of interest. A young Hollander, van Lier, was appointed minister at Cape Town in 1786 and in a short ministry of seven years did much to arouse his flock to the necessity of missionary work among the Hottentots and slaves, and to encourage the establishment of a missionary society in Holland which would sponsor such work in Africa. In 1794 Michiel Vos returned to the Cape after training for the ministry in Holland and was to set to work at Roodezand about fifty miles to the north of the Cape Town-Stellenbosch axis. Here he devoted himself to stirring the conscience of his own white congregation, persuading farmers to take seriously the work of converting their own slaves (conversion was no longer in practice a step towards manumission), and generally making missionary activity a normal part of the life of his pastorate.

In 1787 Bishop Reichel of the *Unitas Fratrum* visited the Cape and, after conversations with van Lier and others, became convinced that the time was ripe for a formal application for permission to reopen the Moravian station. This time the Brethren were given permission to administer the sacraments as well as to preach to the Hottentots, provided that they did not set up their missions in an area where congregations of the official Church already existed. In November 1792 Brothers Marsveld, Schwinn, and Kühnel arrived in the colony and made their way to Schmidt's old settlement at Genadendal.

Dramatic and sentimental stories are told about the old woman, Lena, who had been converted by Schmidt and who had remained near Genadendal. The sober truth is perhaps even more startling. Not only had Lena retained some vague memories of what she had been taught, but there were a great many other Hottentots who remembered Schmidt and who had some sort of belief. Some had continued to say their prayers. Others had taught their children to pray. It may reasonably be conjectured that their beliefs were garbled versions of the faith Schmidt had taught and that their prayers were said with no very clear idea of what was meant by them.

The new Brethren were all older than Schmidt had been and they were a team. They soon re-established the station and created a new Christian congregation and community. The mission expanded fairly rapidly, perhaps more rapidly than the Brethren really desired. Hottentots flocked to school and to church. The English government, which soon came to administer the Cape, encouraged them to settle on the mission stations. New centres had to be opened to cope with the numbers. The Brethren had each been trained in a trade and they were able to make most of the things they needed. They also taught the Hottentots in various crafts in addition to reading and writing and the principles of Christianity. A measure of organization and administration was forced upon them in spite of the resentment which the Brethren themselves felt at the necessity. So effective was their work that they were invited to provide chaplains for Hottentots who enlisted in the army—an invitation they were unable to accept. Right up to the end of the governorship of Lord Charles Somerset, in 1826, this expansion and the consequent growth in administrative complexities continued. Then the abolition of slavery, the bitterness over pass laws, anti-Hottentot feeling in the colony generally, and the unpopularity of missions slowed down the growth of the Moravian work. But by the middle of the nineteenth century they possessed seven well-established stations with a total of 7,100 members and served by twenty-eight missionaries and thirteen "native helpers".

None of this expansion was originally part of the Moravian plan. What they had had in mind was the patient, gradual gathering together of converts who had been thoroughly prepared, genuinely converted, and willing to accept the discipline of living together in a Christian community. Thus Moravian mission stations became communities on the Herrnhut pattern. It seems that this, again, was a matter of accident rather than policy. If the Hottentots were to be taught they must cease to be nomads. If they were to be kept faithful they must be looked after. Enclosed settlements came into being and, once this had happened, the memory and the exemplar of Herrnhut was too strong to be resisted. The settlements became villages where the dignity of labour, the skills of the trades themselves, elementary general education, and standards of civilized living were all taught, together with the gospel. They were disciplined communities where Hottentots were encouraged to live their whole lives so that the moral standards might be maintained. Fortuitously there was developed a missionary strategy which aimed at the creation of communities into which the heathen were to be brought. They were to be converted out of one kind of society, culture, and life into another, and in these new communities, these *ecclesiolae*, they were to remain for the rest of their days. The Moravian pattern worked so well in practice that it became the ideal for many other Christians. It was to be a permanent factor in South African Church history.

3. The Dutch Reformed and Anglican Establishments

In 1793 revolutionary and republican France declared war on a coalition of European states including Holland. Holland was invaded and some of the Dutch sympathized with the invaders. By 1795 the Prince of Orange had fled the country and the "Batavian Republic" was set up as a French satellite. The Prince of Orange took refuge in England. He was anxious that British forces should protect Dutch colonies. England was equally anxious to prevent France from closing the sea route to India. The Prince of Orange ordered the authorities at Cape Town to surrender to the British. A British expedition arrived at the Cape in June 1795. They found a curious situation in the colony.

The princes of Orange had been stadtholders (effective heads of the Dutch state) since it first became independent. But revolutionary ideas had made their appearance at the Cape long before 1795. At the same time as the Company declined, the colony was rapidly expanding. For the farmers who pushed the frontiers eastward authority in Cape Town was at best an irrelevance and at worst a restricting nuisance. By the last decade of the eighteenth century white settlers had moved as far east as the Great Fish River. There had been trouble with the African tribes. The administration could not effectively protect the settlers from raids. Indeed its principal concern was to prevent any further expansion. Moreover the Company was drawing in its horns, recalling garrisons, abandoning guard-posts. Republican ideas dribbled through to the Cape and were clothed with the more popular local substance of grievances against the administration in Cape Town. Two little republics were set up in the eastern part of the Colony. Sluysken, the governor, therefore found himself badly hampered in his dealings with the British forces. The Company's authority was being questioned. The Prince of Orange could not command the undivided loyalty of even the administration. Sluysken opposed the British landing but was soon compelled to surrender.

The first British occupation of the Cape lasted from 1795 to 1803. By the terms of the capitulation Britain undertook to maintain the *status quo* in the colony and even to grant the colonists a freedom in commercial matters which the Company had not been prepared to grant. The new rulers were also to preserve and maintain the privileges of the Dutch Reformed Church. It will be a convenience to talk of an "establishment" or an "established Church", meaning the Church recognized and protected by the law of the colony. In this sense the Dutch Church had been the established Church in the days of the Company. In this sense it was to continue to be "established" during the occupation. But, of course, the British administration could not undertake to maintain the old relationship between the Church in the Cape and the *classis* at Amsterdam, which was now within the territory of a hostile republic. Nor was it any longer possible to defend the establishment on the basis of the maxim *cuius regio*, for the burghers were now required to take an oath of allegiance to George III (for so long as the occupation should last). The request of the Prince of Orange had provided the pretext upon which Britain had occupied the Cape, but the ruler of the colony was plainly the king of England. The religion of the ruler was no longer the religion of the territory. For the king, who was already officially an Anglican in England and a Presbyterian in Scotland, this was perhaps no very great problem. But the members of the Cape Church had to get used to the idea of being protected by a government which did not share their religious beliefs. Moreover the Church in the Cape had, in the course of the eighteenth century, begun to take the first steps towards independence of Amsterdam. Repeated requests had been made to the Company for permission to set up a presbytery, or some other single assembly, for the whole Church in the colony. Eventually, about the middle of the eighteenth century, this permission had been given. The Cape Church was in a position, in spite of the fact that the meeting lacked the full status of a presbytery or *classis*, to express its corporate mind and take steps towards its eventual independence. But when the Church in the Cape had attempted to assert its own authority there was a sharp clash with the Amsterdam *classis* which resulted in the disbanding of the Church assembly in 1759.

These first tentative steps towards the creation of a local presbytery did nothing to free the Church from the control of the civil administration. Great Britain, therefore, inherited (and undertook to maintain) an establishment in which the government exercised considerable authority in all Church matters, in the payment and appointment of clergy, and in the machinery of Church administration. It is no doubt true that by the end of the eighteenth century religious issues no longer roused the same bitter and passionate feelings as they had done in the previous century. But since the colonists were in any case impatient of government there were occasions on which the Dutch settlers found it galling in the extreme to belong to a Church which was established under English rule.

On the whole the government seems to have been tactful in its intervention in Church matters, but in Graaff Reinet there was a delicate situation which needed careful handling. Here, in the most easterly region of the colony, the republicans refused to accept British rule for nearly a year after Sluysken's surrender. The local minister, von Manger, had abandoned the republicans and taken an oath to the British king. The government found itself attempting to reinstate a clergyman, whom his congregation did not want, in a district which did not yet recognize British rule.

This curious establishment, under a foreign ruler with a different religion, worked well enough so long as it was merely a temporary arrangement. The Anglican Church took no root in the colony. The only Anglican clergymen who came to the Cape were the chaplains appointed to serve the naval or military forces of the occupation. They were strictly instructed that their ministrations were to be confined to the garrison and to British officials. No attempt was made to create Anglican churches or congregations. Anglican missions were not even considered. There was some conflict nevertheless. The monopoly of the Dutch Church and its teaching on baptism were both infringed when Anglican clergy took it upon themselves to baptize slaves or

Hottentots. Again and again the Reformed authorities protested and the English government upheld their protests.

In 1803 the Cape passed once more into Dutch hands. In the previous year the peace of Amiens called a temporary halt to the wars with France. Napoleon Bonaparte had become First Consul. Both sides needed a breathing space and Amiens provided it. One of the terms of the peace was that the Cape should be handed over to the Dutch Batavian Republic. The claims of the Prince of Orange were ignored.

The government of the colony now became the responsibility of two men, General Janssens, the new governor, and Commissioner-General de Mist, a member of the council which had succeeded to the administrative responsibilities of the Company. De Mist, who remained in the colony for nearly two years, was a man of considerable brilliance. He was a disciple of the French philosophers and the Enlightenment. It was his job to create a new constitution and new administrative machinery for the Cape. This he did, tidying up some of the anomalies, defining the duties of officials more clearly, endeavouring to prevent corruption and removing the more cumbersome features of the Company's system of administration. His new regulations for the Cape also affected the Dutch Church.

In a preliminary general survey of conditions at the Cape, written in 1802 before the actual transfer of the colony, de Mist had displayed his quick grasp of the situation. He enunciated the general principle that no community could exist without making provision for the maintenance of religion, but he was not merely restating the old belief that the State Church must possess a monopoly in religion. Once he began to implement his policy he was prepared to give the protection of the law to Reformed, Lutherans, Anglicans, and others. He spoke most highly of the work being done by the Moravians. The Batavian Republic, he believed, must make provision for the spiritual as well as the material needs of its subjects. It was a "Supreme Being" rather than the God of Calvin whom the State had a duty to support. And this duty was not imposed by any abstract notion of what was due to the deity. It was a necessity to be measured in terms of the hard social and political realities of the colonial situation.

There were only two Churches recognized in the colony—the Dutch Reformed and the Lutheran. The Lutherans had one minister in Cape Town. The Dutch had, besides two retired clergymen, three who worked in Cape Town and five for the rest of the colony. This was not nearly enough, de Mist argued, to civilize and spiritualize the rough, half-savage white settlers. The rebellion at Graaff Reinet was a result of the corruption of moral sense. The men of Graaff Reinet, with their talk of the tricolour and the republic, would have regarded this as a bitter judgment coming, as it did, from the representative of the new order. But de Mist found little to admire in the incipient separatism of the farmers in the east. He thought it might be their diet (too much meat) which made them such barbarians! He was quite certain that more clergymen and more schoolmasters would help them to become more civilized. Therefore the State ought to continue to support and extend the work of the Church in order to make better and more enlightened citizens. It is clear that he regarded the Church as, in a sense, a political agency—in spite of the fact that since 1795 the old relationship between Church and State in Holland had been dissolved. The government was anxious to control the Church at the Cape because it saw the Church as an invaluable instrument in the work of governing the colony.

This desire is reflected in de Mist's Church regulations of 1804. The Dutch Reformed Church is specifically declared to be no longer the State Church but, since it was by far the largest religious body and was the helpmeet of the government, it was given certain privileges. Privileges from the State, however, turned out to be restrictions and hindrances in some respects. No services might be held without the governor's permission. No court of the Church, consistory or synod, might assemble unless the government were represented by political commissioners. No minister might be appointed without the consent of the government. The general effect of the regulations was to subordinate the Church more firmly than ever to the Cape administration even though, at the same time, it was given rather more independence from Amsterdam. The general Church assembly or synod, the single body to represent all the Cape congregations, was to be revived and given wider powers than it had possessed before. But, as it happened, it did not actually meet for the first time until twenty years later.

In the meantime, in 1806, the Cape was again occupied by Great Britain. Napoleon had made himself emperor of the French. Hostilities had been renewed and Britain again felt it necessary to secure the sea route to India. Janssens opposed the landing of the British forces but was driven back inland and eventually surrendered. In the three years during which the Dutch had held the Cape the frontiers had been further extended, and the general problems of administration made more complex in consequence.

For eight years the British administration of the colony was an "occupation" by right of conquest only. Until 1814, when Napoleon had been defeated and was sent to exile on Elba, Britain had no absolute title to the Cape. During these years the situation as regards the Churches was much as it had been during the first occupation. The Dutch Church was once more guaranteed its property and privileges. Anglican clergy, who were again military and naval chaplains, were not allowed to minister to anyone who was not a member of the garrison or the administration. When there was a recurrence of friction between English and Dutch clergy, the acting-governor and commander-in-chief (General Baird) showed a great deal of sympathy towards the Dutch clergy and compelled the Anglican chaplains to toe the line. But after the formal cession of the Cape to Great Britain by the peace treaty of 1814 the Anglican clergy were allowed more liberty. Baird had, in any case, disapproved of the Dutch law which allowed marriages to be conducted by civil officials. The new administration insisted that this was a function proper only to ordained ministers of religion. After 1814 Anglican clergymen were given the right to call banns as well as perform the marriage service. It was a recognition of the fact that the Dutch Church was no longer the only body with a real pastoral interest in the homes and families of settlers. The British administration of the Cape had ceased to be a mere "occupation"; it had become a "colonization".

The development of the British section of the colony's population was given further impetus by the arrival of the 1820 settlers.

About 3,500 people arrived from Great Britain under a scheme designed to alleviate unemployment, and they were settled in the eastern Cape. The centre of gravity of the English part of the population shifted to the east. The frontier districts became more thickly populated with white settlers. The British sector of the colony received an addition which doubled its strength. And the Cape became rather more obviously British territory.

By 1830, then, the Cape was not only legally a British possession; it had also acquired a settled British population which regarded the colony as its permanent home. As a result of this a very curious situation arose for the English and Dutch Churches. The English Church was the official Church of the government. The Dutch Church was the official Church of the colony. There was a sense in which both could be regarded as "established", though neither was strictly "the established Church".

We have already seen that after 1804 the Dutch Reformed Church was no longer established in the strict sense, though it continued to occupy a privileged position, to receive financial support, and to be restricted by government control. This continued to be the case after 1814. The general Cape synod or assembly, provided for in de Mist's regulations, did not meet until 1824. The colony was by this time a British possession. Nevertheless de Mist's rules were applied. Two commissioners representing the Crown attended the sessions. They took an active part in affairs and reported on the meeting to the civil authorities. The decisions of the assembly were sent to England to receive the Royal Assent—though, in fact, nothing seems to have been heard of them again.

Rather more serious in practice was the fact that all official connection between the Cape and Holland had been broken. The number of clergy serving the Reformed Church in the colony declined because it was no longer so easy to import ministers from what had until recently been the mother country but was now a foreign power. The government, however, took its responsibilities towards the Church seriously. It tried to find suitable ministers for appointment in Scotland when candidates for vacant posts were not forthcoming from Holland. At the synod of 1824 the suggestion was made that there should be some sort of official union with the Church of Scotland. It is easy to imagine that the government would have welcomed this solution of its difficulties. The Scots Church was Presbyterian and Calvinist, as the Cape Reformed Church was. The Scots Church was the established Church of part of the United Kingdom, just as the Dutch Church was, in a sense, the established Church in the colony. Such a union would have made everything very much tidier and simpler. But the scheme was not pressed. Scottish ministers continued to be employed in Cape congregations and exerted a considerable influence upon the Dutch Church. But there was no union.

There were quite as many inconsistencies and anomalies in the position of the English Church in the colony. It was in no real sense the established Church. Yet the governor of the colony acted as "ordinary"—that is to say, he exercised all the disciplinary functions and jurisdiction (but not the spiritual authority) of an Anglican bishop. On the other hand the clergy received their licences from the Bishop of London. After 1810 civil or colonial chaplains were appointed as well as military and naval chaplains. It was their job to care for the spiritual welfare of the civil officials and the growing number of English-speaking settlers, just as it was the job of the military chaplains to care for the garrisons. Colonial chaplains were appointed and paid by the Colonial Office in London. They had no parishes, no areas for which they were specifically responsible. The churches in which they ministered were built by a very curious scheme in which the building was made the property of a joint-stock company. Shares were sold to anyone who would buy them, whether they were Anglicans (or even Christians) or not, and the proceeds were used to pay the cost of erecting the church. Shareholders then received a dividend paid out of pew-rents. Each such church was given a legal existence by an ordinance of the colonial government and each church and congregation could be regarded as separately "established" by law. There was no such thing as a single Anglican Church for the colony. Each congregation was regarded as a part of the Church of England as by law established in England.

Nor were these two semi-established Churches the only two which received government assistance. The policy adopted by de Mist was continued. Government grants were given to several denominations for the support of their clergy. In 1832 the Dutch Reformed Church in the colony had eighteen congregations, nineteen clergymen, and a subsidy of £4,200 per annum. The Anglican Church had six congregations and six clergymen. Their grant was £1,850. The Roman Catholics and Scottish Presbyterians each had one clergyman in the colony and were given £200 per annum.

4. *Vanderkemp and Philip of the London Missionary Society*

The eighteenth century is still reckoned as a period in which the combined effects of rationalism, laxness, and a distrust of "enthusiasm" made the Church somewhat immobile. But the eighteenth century was also the period of the Evangelical revival. Men like Whitefield and the Wesleys campaigned for the conversion of England and in doing so adopted a course of action which eventually led to a separation between their followers and the established Church. Other Anglican clergymen shared their "enthusiasm", their emphasis upon conversion and the need for vivid personal religious experience, but remained within the Church of England. These movements, within and without the established Church, which shared a common conviction of the importance of personal conversion and of high standards of morality and which laid great emphasis upon the redeeming death of Christ, also shared a concern for the taking of the gospel to the heathen abroad.

The Evangelical revival thus led to the founding of many missionary societies, of which one of the most famous was the London Missionary Society. This body was to be undenominational and its agents were to preach the Gospel without propagating any particular form of Church order or government. Its founders planned to evangelize the island of Tahiti and then turn their attention to Africa, Tartary, Astrachan, Surat, Malabar, Bengal, Coromandel, and Sumatra. One suspects that the glamorous sound of exotic and romantic names was not without its appeal to these respectable Evangelicals. The word "mission" was full of the sound and colour of drama and heroism. Perhaps "the Cape of Good Hope" itself sounded romantic in 1795, the year the L.M.S. was inaugurated and the colony was occupied for the first time by British troops. At any rate it soon took precedence in the Society's plans over Tartary and Coromandel. In 1799 there arrived at the Cape the first L.M.S. missionary, Johannes Theodorus Vanderkemp.[1]

Vanderkemp, who had been trained in medicine at Edinburgh, was a Hollander by birth and was welcomed by the L.M.S. as the ideal man for work in what had been till very recently a Dutch possession. In early life he had apparently been an unbeliever and something of a rake, but his interest in Christianity was quickened by the death of his wife and daughter in a boating accident and culminated in a vivid conversion. In the end he offered his services to the Society and arrived at the Cape with three other missionaries, two of whom made their way to the northern frontiers of the colony.

Vanderkemp himself first attempted to work amongst the people of Gaika (Ngqika), an African chief on the eastern frontier. He met with no success at all. White settlers had by this time come into permanent contact with African tribes. The frontier was in a most disturbed condition. Xhosa raids on white farms and punitive expeditions on the part of the colonists were continually exacerbating the tension between the two races. The Boers of the colony's eastern districts became more and more impatient of government control, arguing that the administration was unable to protect them but was determined to prevent them from protecting themselves. For these and other reasons Vanderkemp's sole harvest, after a year of missionary endeavour was a single convert. He abandoned Gaika's people and moved back into the colony to Graaff Reinet, then very much a centre of Boer dissatisfaction and resentment. Here Vanderkemp, now assisted by a missionary called Read, began to work amongst Hottentots. At this stage he was still presumably popular amongst even the settlers of Graaff Reinet, for he was invited to become their minister. But the Hottentots had won his sympathy. He appealed to the government for support in the creation of a missionary "Institution" which would be an instrument for the conversion of the Hottentots, provide a place of refuge for the miserably

[1] The name is sometimes written van der Kemp, and the doctor himself spelled it in several different ways.

poor Hottentot squatters, and a means of pacifying bands of Hottentot terrorists on the frontier. The governor was sympathetic,
though he also advised Vanderkemp that the international situation did not make that moment a very propitious one for new
enterprises in the colony. But Vanderkemp went ahead nevertheless. The "Institution" was begun near what is now Port
Elizabeth. Opposition from the colonists, sickness, every kind of
small disaster, made its survival doubtful from the start. The
uncertainty which followed the departure of the British troops
finally put an end to the brief settlement and after the arrival of
Janssens and de Mist the Institution was re-established further
inland at "Bethelsdorp".

It is terribly difficult to make any proper assessment of Vanderkemp's work at Bethelsdorp. Vanderkemp was so hated by the
colonists that it is hardly possible to find unbiassed evidence on
which to base the assessment. He was certainly an eccentric, a
visionary, and an ideologue. Such a man must be suspect on a
rough, dangerous frontier. Vanderkemp wanted to provide land-
less Hottentots with a place of refuge. The colonists, who wanted
the Hottentots as farm labourers, denounced Bethelsdorp as a nest
of idleness and vice. Vanderkemp tried to identify himself with
his flock, dressing, eating, and living like them, and marrying a
Malagasy slave. He was accused of lowering himself and all other
white men and even of dragging the Hottentots down and of
treating the Hottentot as though he were Rousseau's noble savage.

Vanderkemp claimed that it was his definite policy to insist
that every Hottentot at Bethelsdorp should work for his living,
but the station failed to become a busy, self-supporting community
like the Moravian settlements. Vanderkemp complained that the
land was poor but the vagrant Hottentots knew a good thing when
they saw it. And Vanderkemp seems to have lacked the ability
(or perhaps the sternness) to insist that those who would not work
must go without.

Vanderkemp died in 1812 having earned for the London Missionary Society, whether justly or unjustly, an unenviable reputation in the colony. After he died the Society, feeling that something must be done to maintain discipline in the Cape stations,
decided to appoint a superintendent to have oversight of all the

work in South Africa. First a clergyman called John Campbell
made a tour of inspection, and he was joined by George Thom,
whose report on the work being done at Bethelsdorp was far from
complimentary.

Eventually, in 1820, Dr John Philip was appointed to take
charge of the work at the Cape. He was physically tough, with a
keen active mind and a strong, obstinate spirit. If Vanderkemp
was a disciple of Rousseau, Philip was a disciple of Adam Smith.
He was the son of a weaver. His ability was shown by the fact
that by the time he was twenty he had become works manager of
a Dundee power mill. His social concern was shown by the fact
that within a very few months he had resigned again because he
could not stomach the conditions under which children were
compelled to work in his factory.

In South Africa Philip was principally concerned in two matters which laid him open to the charge of interfering in politics.
One was the continual unrest between black and white on the
frontiers. The other was the condition of the Hottentots within
the colony. To Philip both were parts of the one important issue,
how to secure *just* treatment for the aboriginal population of
southern Africa.

This was a period in which the Hottentots seemed to constitute
a grave problem. These people really only had a choice between
being farm labourers or vagrants. There was no other niche in
Cape society which they could occupy. Farm labour was not well
paid. The work was hard and, though such work would give a
man and his family some security and some reward in kind, the
conditions did not appeal to a race whose immemorial custom
was to live off the land. Nor was the legal status of the Hottentot
population clear. They were neither slaves nor citizens. Pass laws
might be created to check vagrancy. Contracts of service might
be registered to check desertion. The Hottentots remained un-
repentant and nomadic.

It is true that the abolition of the slave trade in 1807 had en-
hanced the value of the Hottentot to the farmer. There had never
been a vast slave population in the colony. Now no more could
be imported. The farmer was dependent upon the Hottentot for
labour. A Pass Ordinance of 1809 had attempted to compel the

Hottentot to work for the farmer, but at the same time it had recognized his legal existence and gave him a status and some rights. In 1812 an Apprenticeship Ordinance permitted farmers to employ Hottentot children as indentured labour. Farmers who found themselves supporting hordes of Hottentot children in return for the labour of the Hottentot *paterfamilias* felt that they had a right to insist that some of the children should work for them. The system was open to abuse, however, for few Hottentot children would know their own exact age and the apprenticeship might be stretched to cover an undue period.

The L.M.S. missionaries, under Vanderkemp's leadership, had become the champions of the Hottentot. Mission stations gave the Hottentots an alternative to either farm labour or vagrancy. It is possible that, at one time, as high a proportion as one third of the total Hottentot population were living on missions. The farmers came to regard the missionaries as the villains who were responsible for the shortage of labour. The missionaries, in their turn, began to hear stories about the cruelties inflicted on Hottentots by their employers. In 1812, after Vanderkemp's death, a court in the eastern Cape (which has gone down in South African history as the "Black Circuit") heard a whole series of complaints. James Read, Vanderkemp's colleague, was really responsible for pressing the charges. Farmers were appalled to find that they could be compelled to appear in court at the instance of mere Hottentots. The Hottentots themselves must have realized that, if they could not make the charges stick, their position would be far worse than it had ever been before. It is highly probable that false evidence was given by both sides. Only a very few of the charges were proved. Missionaries were henceforward to be regarded as troublemakers and agitators.

As superintendent, Philip, conscientious, officious, humanitarian, was probably better informed about conditions in the colony than any government official or colonist. He received reports from the stations and made a point of travelling about a good deal. He was appalled by the conditions under which the Hottentots lived and he believed that unjust laws were responsible for their maltreatment. He invoked the support of his Evangelical friends in England and a commission of inquiry into conditions at the Cape was appointed. In 1828 the government issued the notorious "Ordinance 50" with which Philip's name has always been linked in execration. Vagrancy was no longer punishable. The Hottentots could give or withhold their labour. All free persons of colour were to have the same legal rights as white colonists. This ordinance could not be altered without the approval of the imperial government.

In the same year Philip published a book called *Researches in South Africa* which continued to assert the charges of cruelty and injustice which had originated with Read and Vanderkemp. The book was informed and factual but perhaps exaggerated in places. A libel action followed, which came near to ruining Philip both financially and in his standing in the colony.

Philip was also concerned with the African population of the sub-continent. The fact that the L.M.S. had developed to the north as well as the east of the colony meant that, as superintendent, he was very much concerned with frontier conditions. And again it seemed to Philip that the white colonists were largely to blame for the continual unrest and sporadic warfare. The so-called "Treaty System" by which chiefs on the frontiers were recognized as independent rulers (with the implication that the British administration would recognize their right to punish marauding colonists) was regarded as another typical result of Philip's influence with important Evangelicals at home. And when, in the 1830s, Charles Grant (Lord Glenelg) became Colonial Secretary it looked as though the missionaries had won. Grant was the son of one of the outstanding Evangelical pioneers of the previous generation. Colonial policy was in the hands of missionaries and their friends.

One other matter needs to be noted. Philip believed that if there was ever to be an answer to the Hottentot problem, other than vagrancy or forced labour, they must be trained and equipped to fulfil other roles. The Hottentots ought, therefore, to live on mission stations and other "places of refuge" until they had become sufficiently civilized to take their place as full citizens of the colony.

The man who devised this scheme of limited and temporary *apartheid* has been reviled as a liar, a slanderer, a prejudiced and insidious politician. He has been lauded as the first and most vigorous champion of the underprivileged people of South Africa. Perhaps the fairest and least emotionally distorted judgment sees him as an honest, sensible man, too far ahead of his contemporaries, sometimes making mistakes, but genuinely concerned with finding the just and practical solution. As he grew older Philip took less part in openly political affairs. He retired to one of the eastern Cape mission stations and lived there quietly until his death in 1851.

5. 1820 and the beginnings of Methodism

John Wesley died only a few years before the first British occupation of the Cape. Up to his death he had protested vigorously that he had no intention of leaving the Church of England or of creating a rival denomination. Nevertheless he left behind him what was virtually a Methodist Church. Wesley lived in an England where formalism and aridity were the dangers, where enthusiasm was suspect, and reason was the great standard by which all things were to be judged. The rapid growth of industrialization created vast urban districts in which a new proletariat lived in degrading conditions. The established Church could create new parishes only by means of a procedure so clumsy and complicated that it was better left alone. The Dissenters were restricted and controlled by law and were no more inclined to undertake the conversion of the new slums than were the general run of Anglican clergymen.

But Wesley was willing to accept the challenge. He was prepared, if necessary, to regard the world as his parish. He preached up and down England. He aimed at conversion rather than at reasoned, intellectual discussion. When he had made converts from the lower classes he could not leave them to sink or swim as individuals: he formed societies. He could not be contained by the parochial system and he was continually intruding into the parishes of other Anglican priests. He provoked their hostility and they hated his enthusiasm. He had no intention of forming "another denomination" and he urged his followers to remain within the Church of England. Yet, step by step, and sometimes almost by accident, the separation was made. By 1795, the year of the first British occupation of the Cape and four years after Wesley's death, Methodism was virtually another Church.

Methodism appeared amongst the garrison during this first occupation, to the great distaste of the authorities. Later, after the second occupation, the first really active Methodist minister arrived at the Cape and was refused the governor's permission for the holding of services. But this minister, Barnabas Shaw, was primarily a missionary. He had been sent to South Africa to convert the heathen. A missionary of the L.M.S. persuaded him that he ought to go and work amongst the people of Namaqualand beyond the Orange River. Lord Charles Somerset, the governor, did not refuse Shaw permission to leave the colony, but he advised him very strongly to remain within its frontiers, actually offering to appoint him minister of one of the Dutch Reformed Church congregations. Shaw persisted and was reluctantly granted his permit.

In the early nineteenth century missionaries simply pitched their tents casually, haphazardly, wherever there were suitable sites with water, food, and heathen to preach to. Barnabas Shaw was not at all perturbed by the fact that he could not speak the language of the heathen. He knew a little rudimentary Dutch, and so did some of them. He stopped his ox-wagon, unpacked, and began to convert people.

It is possible to make out an indictment against all the early missionaries on the grounds that they possessed no strategy, did not plan ahead, were inept and ignorant in their attitude to African traditions and beliefs.[1] It is even true that there were early missionaries who thought that some of the aboriginal peoples had no religion of their own. Plainly they were not (and probably could not be) adequately prepared for what they were going to meet. They must have felt that they had arrived in a looking-glass world where none of the normal rules applied. The extraordinary thing is that so much of this makeshift missionary activity succeeded at all. By 1826 Barnabas Shaw had established a thriving station with a permanent Christian community and from this station there soon grew other centres for evangelism.

This was the beginning of Methodist missions in South Africa,

---

[1] See e.g. D. Williams, *The Missionaries on the Eastern Frontier of the Cape Colony, 1799–1853*. Unpublished thesis, University of the Witwatersrand, Ph.D., 1959.

but the real period of growth for Methodism does not start until after the arrival of the 1820 settlers. The governor, Lord Charles Somerset, had been pressing the government in England to send settlers to the colony in the hope of increasing the white population of the frontier districts. The spread of white settlers eastward and of African tribes south-westward had brought the two races into more permanent contact and frequent conflict. An attempt was made to halt white expansion at the Fish River and the African expansion a little further north and east at the next river valley (the Keiskamma), leaving a no-man's-land in between. But this was no real solution. Neither side was really prepared to honour the frontier. What the colony needed was a denser and more stable white population on the eastern frontier.

Nevertheless the government in London does not at first seem to have favoured assisted emigration to the colonies, even when men who were unemployed in England were emigrating of their own accord to other, non-British, territories. But at last the government asked Parliament for the necessary money in 1819 and the money was voted. The settlers came and, though some of them returned home, the majority remained to provide a settled British population for the eastern Cape and so changed the whole balance of the colony's population generally.

What happened after the settlers had been landed at what is now Port Elizabeth, taken inland, and left to get on with the job of settling, is best described by William Shaw, a twenty-two-year-old Methodist minister:

> After a while a great variety of fragile and grotesque-looking huts or cottages began to arise. These were generally built in the style called by the settlers "wattle and daub". A space of ground was marked off, according to the views of the future occupant of the structure, large enough for one or two rooms. . . . At first there was no plank for doors, or glass for windows: hence a mat or rug was usually hung up in the void doorway . . . and a piece of white calico, nailed to a small frame of wood and fastened into two or three holes left in the walls for the purpose, admitted light into the dwelling during the day, when the wind rendered it inconvenient to keep these spaces open. . . . The floors of these dwellings were usually made of clay. . . . I have described the better class of

structure erected by the settlers at the beginning; but there were
many whose first attempts were miserable failures, and hardly
served to protect them from the weather. Some, taking advantage
of particular spots favourable to their purpose, thought they
saved themselves labour by digging out holes, and burrowing in
the ground, placing a slight covering over their excavations. . . .[1]

Shaw had been invited to the Cape as chaplain to a group of
Methodist families, most of whom came from London, and he
settled with them in what was to become the village of Salem a
few miles from Grahamstown, which was then the headquarters
of the military garrison in the eastern part of the colony. The
Fifth Frontier War had not long before been fought across the
territory in which the settlers now found themselves. The burnt-
out ruins of occasional farmhouses were not only a reminder of
the uncertainties of the frontier, they were also almost the only
signs of any sort of civilization. There was no Church of England
church or chaplain in the eastern Cape at this date. The first such
church to be built was in 1832 at Bathurst, between Grahamstown and the eastern coastline. The first colonial chaplain at
Grahamstown was appointed in 1833. There were missionaries of
the L.M.S., of course, in the area round Algoa Bay. There were
ministers of various denominations in the midlands. But on the
frontier Shaw was the only clergyman and he was prepared, like
Wesley, to take as his parish an area bounded only by the needs
of the people.
He rapidly undertook to care not only for the whole region but
for all races. He learnt "frontier Dutch" in order to be able to
reach the Boers, since he found that the language of the colonists
was already diverging from that of Holland itself. He was careful
to use Wesley's adaptation of the services of the Book of Common
Prayer regularly and frequently because he wished to provide a
form of worship with which Anglicans would feel at home. There
were Methodist soldiers in the garrison at Grahamstown and here
he made the real base for his operations. The foundation stone
of the first church in Grahamstown was laid in December 1821

[1] W. Shaw, *The Story of My Mission in South-Eastern Africa* (Hamilton, Adams & Co. 1860), pp. 4off.

and when it was completed Shaw allowed it to be used by other denominations.

Shaw made full use of the Methodist system of classes and local preachers which was peculiarly suited to the conditions which obtained amongst the settlers. Nor was he concerned with European settlers alone. From Salem the east coast of the continent of Africa stretched out before him as a sort of challenge, for there was hardly a single mission station, as he said, between himself and the Red Sea. He was not content with haphazard missionary squatting and the usual casual lack of strategy. Methodist missions were to be planned and a chain of connected stations set up.

It would be unfair to suggest that Shaw accomplished the whole work. Very little of his time was spent on actual mission stations. Even the demand for missionary expansion did not come from him alone. Letters from Methodist missionaries to their headquarters in London are full of the great need for new stations. Hardly had one new one been set up than the missionaries on the frontier were beginning to talk of planning yet another. Wesleyville was established in 1823, Mount Coke in 1825, Butterworth in 1827, Morley in 1829, Clarkebury and Buntingville in 1830, and Shawbury and Palmerton a little later. Across the Kei River and right into the heart of independent "Kaffirland" stretched this first really coherent systematic missionary achievement in the sub-continent. At a time when other Churches were doing little or nothing, Shaw had laid the foundations for a properly thought out attack on heathenism. By 1860 there were 132 Methodist missionaries at work in the area and their flock numbered close on 5,000.

It must not be thought that this rapid expansion of Methodism went unnoticed or unchallenged. When, tardily and at length, the Anglicans began to make some sort of provision for the eastern Cape there was a good deal of tension between the two bodies. Colonial chaplains were not, on the whole, an inspiring body of men. There were one or two who were good and faithful pastors who would have done credit to the Christian Church anywhere and in any generation. A few were honest if dull. But some were pompous and complacent, and others were rogues. Worst of all

was the notorious Dr Halloran who was not a clergyman at all
but had forged his credentials so as to obtain the appointment.

In the eastern part of the colony some chaplains relied upon
the vestiges of establishment to bolster up their own position.
The Dutch Reformed Church had no dominating position such
as it possessed further west. This was the "English" part of the
colony. It was easy for colonial chaplains to argue that they represented the established Church and that Methodist ministers were
mere dissenters. The echoes of the bitterness aroused in England
by Wesley's attempts to reach the unconverted were often heard
very clearly indeed in the colony.

Even Methodists working in other parts of the country were
not entirely happy with the rapid expansion of missions in the
east. Like the L.M.S. the Methodists had developed a two-
pronged growth—one prong to the north and west, the other to
the south-east. But, unlike the L.M.S., the two Methodist
groups had no common origin nor common organization. And
there was some tension and jealousy between them. The western
part of the work, which Barnabas Shaw had started and over
which he exercised a great influence for a very long time, covered
the Cape peninsula and its hinterland and stretched north into
Namaqualand. It was, perhaps, less systematic and less well
organized than the work in the east. It grew more slowly but it
also had needs. Missionaries in the west felt that an undue proportion of the available funds was going to the east. One of them
had told London that the whole 1820 settlement was a mistake
and that William Shaw was deluding his fellow-settlers, giving
them false hopes and persuading them to stay on. Others, later,
were extremely critical of the rapidity with which the chain of
missions expanded. They complained that thoroughness was
being sacrificed to speed.

This criticism was probably unfair. Shaw was anxious to place
a missionary with each important African chief, and he did this
in the 1820s, while the settlers were still relatively enthusiastic
about missions. Later on there were financial difficulties when
stations were destroyed in frontier warfare, settlers ceased to be
sympathetic, and the Methodist Missionary Society was no
longer able to find the necessary money. None of this was Shaw's

fault. It is true that he made serious mistakes. He insisted on retaining an itinerant ministry in the missions and, moreover, men were moved from one station to another too frequently to provide stability and continuity. His educational policy was unsound, in that he tried to set up too elaborate a system with a branch in every station. His resources, in qualified man-power, were simply insufficient to cope with so diffuse an organization. But when all this has been said, and when due allowance has been made for the faithful and imaginative work done by men like Barnabas Shaw in the western colony, William Shaw has still to be recognized as a great figure in South African missionary history.

6. The Dutch Reformed Church and the Great Trek

The Great Trek, the emigration of a large body of Boers from the eastern Cape in the 1830s, is one of the great dramatic landmarks in South African secular history. Its causes have been much debated by the historians, but perhaps the fundamental cause can be put in the form of a paradox. There was not enough government on the eastern frontier, in one sense, and yet, in another, there was too much. Up to the third quarter of the eighteenth century the trek-boer had been allowed to set the pace for colonial expansion. Then had come the frontier or " Kaffir " wars. Government tried to maintain a separation between colonist and tribesman. Attempts were made to stop the farmers from going over the frontier to retrieve stolen cattle. Both the British and the Batavians sent more and more agents to the east until the administration was strong enough to prevent the colonists' unruly behaviour. The second British occupation, in particular, brought a considerable strengthening of the garrison on the frontier.

There could be no doubt of the government's power to enforce its will on the colonists. The Slachter's Nek rebellion (which arose from the refusal of a farmer to answer a charge of ill-treating a Hottentot) ended in the execution of five farmers. The event left an indelible mark on the frontier memory. Missionary, Hottentot, and government had all combined, the myth said, to hang decent white men. And then the government began to tighten up its land laws. Farms became smaller, because it was important to populate the frontier more thickly. The terms upon which farms could be obtained became stiffer. The British settlers came in 1820 and were willing to farm an area far smaller than the Boer considered necessary. We have already seen how the farmers could blame the shortage of labour on the undue influence of the missionaries upon the government. Grants of land to mission stations meant less labour and less land available for the farmer. And, all along, the government demonstrated over and over again that it was just powerful enough to keep its own white subjects in check. It was never powerful enough, or so it seemed, to smash the "Kaffir" menace across the border.

The general unrest had reached such a pitch by the early 1830s that people were openly talking of leaving the colony. Some had already begun to drift away. Small exploratory treks had set out to see which would be the best route for would-be emigrants to take. In December 1834 war broke out along the frontier and the colony was invaded by tribesmen. The governor, Sir Benjamin D'Urban, was newly arrived. He had been sent out to the colony by the Whigs to enforce a policy of retrenchment, to govern under a new constitution, and to tidy up the consequences of the abolition of slavery. Nevertheless when the Africans were driven back by the colonial forces, D'Urban annexed the territory from the Fish to the Kei. But it was not really possible to clear the whole of the Ciskei of tribesmen. Sporadic raids and fighting continued for some time and opinion in the colony and "at home" was sharply divided over D'Urban's policy. South African missionaries were directly concerned in the controversy.

There were really three issues. Was the attack on the colony "unprovoked aggression" or had the tribes been unjustly treated? Should the annexed territory be returned? If not should it be opened for white settlement or be reserved for Africans? Philip was quite clear that the attack had not been provoked, though he was not opposed to the retention of the territory for African occupation under the Crown. The Methodist missionaries were more sympathetic to D'Urban and the colonists' point of view, perhaps because they worked amongst white settlers as well as amongst the tribes beyond the frontier. Philip regarded them as traitors to the non-white peoples. This was probably unfair. It is true that one Methodist had, at an early stage, expressed himself in terms which were exaggeratedly adulatory of the administration's policy. He subsequently retracted and alleged that his views had been misinterpreted. W. B. Boyce, the most prominent Methodist in the Eastern Cape, was markedly sympathetic to D'Urban, but

4

what he actually advocated was not so dissimilar from Philip's point of view. Shaw, who was in England, took a mediating position and would have preferred missionaries to avoid involvement. But the administration made it plain that they preferred Methodists to other missionaries, and to Philip in particular. The Methodists applied for grants of land from the Crown, whereas the L.M.S. men maintained that the chiefs had already given them their land and the annexation could not retrospectively deprive them of it.

Glenelg, the Colonial Secretary, rejected D'Urban's view of the war. The L.M.S. and the Methodist Missionary Society in England supported him. Philip went to London with his version of events and in the end D'Urban was compelled to abandon the new territory. In the colony the settlers believed that Philip and his disciples were largely responsible for what had happened. It was Philip rather than the Methodists who were taken to be typical of missionary opinion. The farmers on the frontier felt that they had been betrayed by the British government because of the meddling missionaries. In August 1836 the first large party of Trekkers left the colony. In groups of various sizes, some independently, others planning to link up at some vague meeting place in the interior, hundreds of farmers and their families slipped over the frontiers.

In a manifesto issued by the ablest of the Trekkers, Piet Retief, it was alleged that the colony was being overrun by Hottentot vagrants. The farmers were being plundered by "Kaffirs" and the government was quite unable to protect them. The emancipation of the slaves and the method of compensating slave owners had meant severe losses for the colonists. And the farmers could no longer support the unjustified odium cast upon them by the missionaries. The Trekkers, said Retief, desired to live at peace with the tribes of the interior. They would enslave no one, but would maintain a proper relationship between master and servant.

With their most precious belongings loaded on to canvas-topped ox-wagons the Trekkers set out from the eastern districts of the Cape. They moved north, across the Orange River and past the Griqua settlement of Philippolis (named after Dr Philip who had founded an L.M.S. station there in 1821). They clashed with

African tribes, grew in numbers, and quarrelled among themselves. They began to experiment with amateur republican constitutions, in which quaint echoes of Cape colonial practice of various vintages were to be found.

The Trek did not remain united for long. Some of the Trekkers pushed on northwards across the Vaal River. Others settled in the area between the Orange and the Vaal. Retief, followed by a couple of thousand, moved eastward, over the Drakensberg mountains, into Natal. There he was murdered by the Zulu chief, Dingane, in the course of negotiations over the purchase of land. The Boers defeated the Zulu armies at the battle of Blood River in December 1838, and a Trekker republic was established between the Drakensberg and the sea, with the village of Pietermaritzburg as its capital. By 1840 it was clear that settlements of emigrant farmers, hundreds of miles from the nearest frontier of the colony, had become a permanent feature of the southern African scene.

From the first the officials of the Dutch Reformed Church had been out of sympathy with the Trekkers. Ministers of the Church advised the farmers most strongly against leaving the colony. A synod of the Dutch Reformed Church, meeting in 1837, deplored the fact that members of the Church were willing to set out for the wilderness "without a Moses or an Aaron". Perhaps the Church authorities found it difficult to think in terms of extending their jurisdiction beyond the boundaries of the colony. Perhaps the Church simply lacked the means to care adequately for the Trekkers and would have preferred, therefore, that the farmers should stay where pastors could be provided. But probably the clergy felt, more than anything else, that the Trek was a foolish defiance of the government.

The Trekkers differed amongst themselves in matters of religion. Some of them were Doppers, a rigidly puritanical group. They clung tenaciously to the older and more conservative customs and beliefs. They even wore distinctive clothes which marked them off from their orthodox and broader brethren. They objected violently to the singing of hymns in the services of the Church. It was not in South Africa alone that hymn-singing was regarded as a departure from the strict Calvinist tradition. In Scotland an

attempt had been made to introduce hymns into the worship of
the Church in 1781 and the attempt had failed.

The Trekkers did all they could to persuade a *predikant* to
accompany them. But neither flattery nor an appeal to a common
race and interests had any effect. The Trekkers began to feel that
the Church had absorbed too much of the outlook of the government. At this date, moreover, no distinction was made by the
Cape Church between white and non-white members. The races
came together even at the communion, though there were some
congregations where "born Christians" communicated first
whilst the Hottentots waited till the end. Once the seeds of suspicion had been sown it would be easy to treat this as yet another
example of the way in which the Church had adopted the "government" and "missionary" point of view.

The tension was somewhat eased in the 1840s when the Cape
Church itself came into conflict with the government over matters
of ecclesiastical discipline. There was growing dissatisfaction with
what was regarded as secular interference in purely spiritual
affairs. Synod and government were at loggerheads and in 1843 a
Church Ordinance was passed which allowed the Dutch Reformed
Church more autonomy than it had possessed before. After 1850
no state aid was provided for new congregations and the Church
was no longer so obviously dependent upon the British rulers.
But the suspicion already existed and it was a long time before it
finally disappeared.

The fact that the Trekkers were accompanied by no accredited
minister of their own Church did not mean that they were entirely deprived of the pastoral ministrations of Christian clergymen. Maritz, leader of one of the parties, took with him his own
brother-in-law, a Hollander, Erasmus Smit, once in the employ
of the London Missionary Society. It was Maritz's intention to
make Smit the official minister of the combined company of
Trekkers, but the Dopper element would not accept him as
predikant and Smit was to be a continual bone of contention.
Only when it became clear, at last, that the Cape Church was not
going to send a clergyman, was Smit allowed to become the
minister of the party which moved into Natal.

There were others besides Smit from whom the Boers sought

the pastoral oversight which they otherwise lacked. By the third decade of the nineteenth century missionaries had begun to work in most quarters of the sub-continent. The northern "prong" of Methodist missionary expansion had been considerably developed. One of the Methodist missionaries, the enthusiastic but individualistic James Archbell, who was at work amongst the Barolong at Thaba 'Nchu, did what he could for the Trekkers when they arrived in his neighbourhood; though Smit feared that his Methodist Arminianism might taint the good Calvinist Boers.

But the missionary who did most to help the Trekkers was an American Presbyterian, Daniel Lindley, who had come to South Africa in 1835 and was working in the territory of Mzilikazi's Matabele near the Vaal River. Mzilikazi was a fugitive from the Zulu power but his own fearsome people were ruled and trained by methods modelled on those of the Zulus themselves. The Trekker party of Cilliers and Potgieter appeared in the neighbourhood and were attacked by the Matabele at Vegkop in October 1836. The Matabele were defeated but they were able to drive off the herds and flocks of the Trekkers, including the oxen which pulled the famous wagons.

Lindley saw the other side of the struggle between Matabele and Boers. He was a witness of a punitive expedition of January 1837 when a kraal near his mission station was attacked by a Boer commando. In November of the same year an even more formidable Trekker force defeated Mzilikazi decisively near Marico in the Transvaal and the Matabele people swept up north into what was later to become Rhodesia. Lindley's position had become very difficult. From the first Mzilikazi had been suspicious of the white man, prepared to allow individuals into his territory on sufferance but determined to oppose any large-scale immigration. After Vegkop and the raid of January 1837 it was virtually impossible for Lindley to continue his missionary work in the general atmosphere of suspicion and mistrust. The wholesale flight of the Matabele in November would, in any case, have put an end to his missionary plans. Lindley decided to move to Natal and joined forces with the Trekkers for the eastward journey. In spite of his very different point of view—his wife had been a vigorous opponent of the slave-trade in America—he quickly made friends with the Boers.

The party arrived in Natal just before the murder of Retief. Zulu armies swept across Natal. White settlers sought refuge where they could, until Blood River led to the establishment of the white republic. The American missionaries moved for a while to the eastern Cape and Lindley apparently began to think in terms of becoming a full-time minister to the Boer community. He seems to have believed that if he could establish himself in the Church of the Natal republic, be accepted by the Trekkers, minister to them and teach them, he could create a secure base for missionary operations and an atmosphere favourable to missions. In 1840 he was invited to Pietermaritzburg by the Volksraad, and the American Board of Missions gave him leave. Erasmus Smit was pensioned off with £45 per annum. But in 1841 the British authorities indicated that they would not recognize Natal as an independent state. There was a period of unrest and confusion and Natal was officially proclaimed a British colony in 1843. Lindley continued his pastorate amongst the Boers, though the more determined of the citizens of the erstwhile republic moved back across the Drakensberg to the Transvaal.

The British government, having decided that it must assume political responsibility for the Trekkers, planned to assume ecclesiastical responsibility for them also. Ds A. Faure, who had expressed himself strongly against the Trek in the first place, was sent by the governor to spend some months in Natal and to order the religious affairs of the Trekkers. Lindley figures largely in the correspondence which resulted from Faure's visit, and he was officially appointed as a clergyman, in the Cape style, by the government in 1844. The documents imply that Faure's visit was not without political complications. Congregations resented prayers for "her gracious Majesty" and there was general opposition to British rule and to Cape parsons who fostered it. Even Lindley lost a good deal of his popularity because he supported Faure. There was, however, a general agreement that ministers must be provided for the emigrants. The Cape Church debated the matter in the synod of 1847. Though nothing was immediately achieved the synod declared its willingness to re-establish relations with the Trekkers.

7. Frontier and Mission

The twenty years between 1836 and 1856 saw startling changes in the map of southern Africa. In the thirties the Cape Colony had been a fairly narrow strip of territory along the south coast from Cape Town in the west to the Fish River in the east. The rest was wild, unmapped interior, swept by roving African tribes displaced by the explosive creation of the Zulu empire on the east coast. By the middle of the sixth decade the frontiers of the Cape had been extended—north to the Orange River, east to the Keiskamma. The colony of Natal, the territory of British Kaffraria, the Orange Free State, and the republics beyond the Vaal River extended white settlement and government to at least twice the area covered in 1836. The land left to independent Africans had shrunk, but several relatively powerful "states" had emerged. Besides the remnant of the Zulu power and Moshesh's Basutoland, there were the row of Griqua states along the northern frontier of the Cape, and Pondoland to the south of Natal. The whole scene had changed. In 1836 it was still just possible to think in fairly simple terms of a "white" colony, surrounded by undefined, fluid "native" tribes. By 1856 southern Africa was a complicated collection of states, black and white, weak and powerful. What has been called "the Balkanization of South Africa" had occurred.

Sir George Grey arrived at the Cape, as governor, in 1854. He began at once to try and persuade the imperial government to tackle the political and diplomatic problems of South Africa. It was not a propitious moment for such an endeavour. The British government, by and large, was anxious to shed its responsibilities in the sub-continent, not to add to them. Those Englishmen who favoured free trade believed that overseas colonies and possessions were a burden to be shed as fast as possible. The optimists believed that British goods and British ships would always be welcome in every part of the world and that there was no need to saddle oneself with political entanglements abroad. Others believed that colonial demands for self-government meant that in a very few years the empire would disappear altogether. The best that could be hoped for was that secession would be managed amicably.

In other ways Grey's advent was more propitious. He was a civilian whereas former governors had been soldiers. He was acquainted with the notion of federation in Australia and New Zealand and he was ready to try the same idea in South Africa. His plan was, in essence, to federate the three British possessions (Natal, the Cape, and British Kaffraria) and the five Boer republics (the Orange Free State and the four republics north of the Vaal). Grey pointed out that he was not only governor of the Cape, he was also high commissioner. The powers and rights of the high commissioner were never clearly defined but Grey seems to have believed that, in some sense, his authority extended over the whole of the sub-continent.[1] He had, therefore, an enormous responsibility for the maintenance of peace even though his authority might not be recognized by Boer or African states. The "native problem" in southern Africa was a single problem. Unrest in one part of an area would lead inevitably to unrest elsewhere. Since the "white" states were small and in many cases hopelessly unstable, they were a constant temptation to African rulers who might feel that they could raid across the frontiers with impunity. Grey also believed that the fragmentation of "white" South Africa was leading to disorder and barbarism.

Grey's arguments fell on deaf ears. Over and over again he attempted to persuade the imperial authorities to approve his plan. From time to time he had some small success in South Africa itself with one or other of the small "white" states. But

[1] I am indebted for information about the office of high commissioner to Mr J. Benyon, lecturer in history at Rhodes University, and at present engaged upon research connected with Basutoland and the high commission.

there was always some reason why the British government rejected his scheme, or some crisis which frightened the rulers of
the South African colonies and republics. The policy of federation remained a dream. Grey was recalled in 1859 because his
schemes were too dangerous. A change of ministry in England
made it possible for him to return in 1860/61, but only on condition that he ceased to press for federation.

Grey had come to the Cape with a reputation as the man who
had solved the "native problem" in New Zealand. He had won
the confidence of the Maori people. He had been largely successful in pacifying the tribesmen by a policy of "civilizing" them.
In this programme of civilization Christian missions had played
a part.

It was natural that Grey should desire to attempt a similar
policy on the eastern frontier. The problem in the Cape was
rather more difficult than in New Zealand. For one thing most of
the African tribesmen lived outside the limits of British territory.
Moreover white settlers in southern Africa were a far smaller
proportion of the total population of the sub-continent than was
the case in New Zealand. But it must not be thought that the
"native problem" in New Zealand had been easy to solve or that
the Maoris were a gentle, docile people easily dominated by the
colonists. Grey had had to deal with fierce and bitter conflicts
between settlers and "natives" and had achieved some remark-
able successes. There was no *prima facie* reason why the same
policy should not succeed in the Cape. Grey planned to lure
African chiefs into voluntary retirement by promising them pen-
sions and to introduce magistrates gradually to take their place.
He hoped to use educational, missionary, and medical institutions
to further his policy and to create wedges of white settlement in
African areas.

About a year after his arrival in the colony Grey proposed that
Christian mission stations should be used to assist in this policy
of civilizing and pacifying the eastern frontier. Grey's was not the
only plan for making use of missions. In Natal one of his contemporaries was following a policy, very different in conception,
but with some similarity in its effects. The administration of
"native affairs" in Natal was largely in the hands of Theophilus

Shepstone, the son of a Methodist missionary. His policy has been described as one of "insulation and segregation". The Africans were to be gathered in vast "locations", each covering an area of several square miles, where they would be able to continue to live in accordance with their own laws and customs and yet learn something of the civilized way of life. In time the Churches would play a part in the organizing of these locations.

By 1851 opposition from the lieutenant-governor of Natal and from the settlers had led to a considerable modification of this original scheme. Shepstone fought hard to retain something of the original conception and he pressed at the same time for the establishment of mission stations in the reserves. It is worth noting, in passing, that he believed that these missions should not teach a denominational Christianity, on the grounds that savages could not be expected to understand subtle theological differences. But his policy of "insulation" had many opponents. European settlers could not bear to think that they were to be barred for ever from large tracts of southern Africa. Shepstone was never allowed to attempt what he really wanted—which would have involved the wholesale migration of African people and might not have been practicable in the end.

In spite of the fact that the "integrationist" Grey was one of those responsible for putting a stop to the policies of the "separationist" Shepstone, there was a sense in which both men believed that mission stations might be an important factor in solving the "native problem". And the kind of mission station which resulted was very much the same in each case. Indeed, the Moravian village settlements, complete with smithy, mill, school, church, and other facilities for a relatively civilized community life; Dr Philip's scheme for places of refuge and a form of limited *apartheid* which should lead in the end to a real integration; Shepstone's programme for Natal; all these had led in practice to much the same end. There were pronounced differences in both political and missionary theory. There were those who believed that separation of black from white was the only way to secure justice for the former or safety for the latter. There were those who believed that the races must live together, either because it was essential that Africans should provide labour for white landowners or because they honestly believed that peaceful co-existence was right and good. In the matter of missionary strategy, again, there were those who believed that the right thing to do was to convert men out of their native and heathen culture and community and settle them in a context where they could absorb civilization and Christianity together. There were others who believed that converts to Christianity should be left in their own native community, should be encouraged to go out as missionaries amongst their own people, and that African tribes and the African way of life should be christianized as a whole.

It was often the case that political "separationism" went with missionary beliefs of the second type. It is easy to see why this should be so. If one maintains that African culture ought to be retained but christianized then it will often seem that the only way to retain the culture is to insulate it from Western influence. But in practice such insulation was never really achieved. Indeed none of the theories, political, theological, social, or economic, was ever quite faithfully reflected in missionary practice. When Grey spoke of civilizing and christianizing Africans by using mission stations to pacify the eastern frontier, he meant something very different from what Shepstone meant when he spoke of mission stations in his reserves. But, in both these cases, the mission stations were settlements where the church was only one of the communal buildings and where elementary education and instruction in manual crafts were an integral part of the missionary endeavour.

When Grey made his proposal it was accepted with alacrity. From the point of view of the ecclesiastical authorities it was a wonderful opportunity to obtain financial support for missions, for Grey promised to finance the undertaking with £40,000, from funds made available to him by the imperial government and £5,000 from the colony. At this time the Anglican Church in the eastern Cape was struggling to start a missionary campaign. Robert Gray, first Anglican bishop of Cape Town, had been appointed in 1848. From the first it was plain to him that the great need was for missions and that the Anglican Church was unlikely to be effective in this field so long as he was the only bishop in southern Africa and responsible for the whole area. By 1853 it had been agreed to create two new bishoprics and in 1854 (the year Sir George Grey arrived as governor) John Armstrong took up residence as bishop of Grahamstown. Strictly speaking Armstrong's jurisdiction did not extend beyond the colony, but one of the reasons behind his appointment was the hope that he would establish missions, as the Methodists had done, throughout the frontier region. When Grey's invitation reached Armstrong he called his clergy together and on their advice agreed to establish four mission stations beyond the frontier—one for each of the principal chiefs in the area.

This was a period of stagnation, if not of disaster, for Methodist missions in the area. Perhaps Methodist resources had been strained by too rapid an expansion in various parts of the world. Frontier wars had led to destruction of mission stations and had alienated settler sympathies. The Methodist Church as a whole had been disrupted by controversies in the 1840s. Mission stations had to be abandoned because there was neither the men nor the money to maintain them. In 1856 James Thomas, one of the leading missionaries on the fontier, was murdered and the position seemed desperate. But a special appeal for funds was made in England and it was soon possible to staff all the surviving stations again. It seemed possible that Grey's plans for a missionary pacification of the territory beyond the frontier might work after all. Some of his funds went to the Methodists also.

But in 1857 came the famous "Cattle-killing" or "National Suicide" of the Xhosa people. African prophets said that if their people killed their cattle and destroyed their crops, the spirits of the ancestors would return on a specified day, give them new and more perfect cattle and endless supplies of food, and drive the white man into the sea. The day came but it brought no triumph with it. The crops and the cattle had been destroyed. The prophecy was not fulfilled. The people were left to starve.

Sir George Grey had tried to provide stocks of food against the inevitable end of the prophecies. There was not enough to go round. The missionaries struggled to feed and care for thousands of the starving. In the end the disaster was too great to be met by any of these measures. The Xhosa people were broken. For a whole generation, until new warriors had grown up, there was a peace of exhaustion along the frontier. Africans came into the colony to look for work. White colonists were settled in the now depopulated areas. By 1866 the frontier of the Cape Colony had reached the Kei River. The power of the chiefs had been broken. Some missionaries rejoiced that good had come out of evil, for the chief's power had been one of the obstacles in the way of their work. John Armstrong's successor as bishop of Grahams-town believed that the Xhosa tragedy had given the Church an opportunity to build a Christian nation out of the wreckage of the heathen tribes.

Beyond the Xhosa lay the Pondos, deeper into the territory across the Kei and further to the north. From 1830, when the station at Buntingville had been founded, Methodist missionaries had played an important part in maintaining contact between the colony and the Pondo people. They were instructed by their missionary society that they were not to meddle in political mat-ters and, in a direct sense, they were careful to obey these instruc-tions. But it was not always easy to obey them in every sense. What might appear to be "politics" to an observer in England might appear to be a matter of necessity or Christian charity at the frontier. In 1824 William Shaw had taken part in a conference between a representative of the Cape government and the African chiefs. Was this meddling in politics? We have already seen how deeply Methodist missionaries were involved in frontier matters in 1835 and 1836. The best of them had then been moved by compassion for homeless Africans and by goodwill to the colonial administration. They deliberately tried to act as intermediaries and came to be used more and more, officially and unofficially, as agents or commissioners of the government with the tribes beyond the Kei. One such missionary, Thomas Jenkins, worked in Pondo-land from 1838 to 1868 and was able to play an important diplo-matic role. It was not always easy to be sure whether this was "politics" or not.

The creation of government agents, commissioners, and resi-dent magistrates was an intermediate stage as it were, in the

process which led eventually to the final annexation of the territory which lay between the Kei and Natal. By and large it was not
only welcomed by missionaries of all denominations, it was
something for which they worked actively. We have already seen
that missionary theory could not always be put into practice
without modification. Practical difficulties compelled even those
who did not want "insulated" mission stations to adopt some of
the features of "insulation". Where missionaries worked amongst
more or less hostile chiefs, mission stations would inevitably
become isolated from surrounding villages. Even where there
was no open hostility, missionaries who required their converts
to abandon such integral parts of African life as polygamy and
witchcraft were compelled to provide a society in which those
converts could live in relative peace and comfort. And if refugees
from African justice came to missionaries and claimed that they
were being persecuted as supposed witches, missionaries very
often believed that they must protect them from their own chiefs.
Under these circumstances it was not surprising that most missionaries longed, and even worked actively, for the day when
British rule, and British order and justice, would cover all
southern Africa.

But the association between missionaries and government was
to lead to a tragic end which no missionary a hundred years ago
could possibly have foreseen. A recent African writer has described the missionaries as the pioneering empire builders.

A successful empire builder lays down laws. Strongly supported
by the army, the missionaries became dogmatic and tough with
us. We were dispossessed of large pieces of land which became
by law "missionary reserves" where only faithful and proved
"followers" were allowed residence at the discretion of the missionaries concerned.[1]

This view of the missionary as the advance agent of white imperialism is now widely held. The missionaries were willing to
co-operate in the "christianization" and pacification of the

[1] T. Matshikiza, "The Role of the Missionary in the Conquest of
South Africa", *Prism,*   63, p. 18.

frontier. They were willing to act as government representatives (officially or unofficially). They were inclined to press for the extension of British rule in the interests of peace and justice. It is easy to see how their actions and principles could be interpreted in a way which would have shocked and appalled them.

8. Livingstone and Exploration

Although the greater part of Livingstone's life was spent outside South Africa itself, he made a dynamic impact on the work of the missionary Church. At ten he was a piecer in a cotton mill, but by sheer indomitable industry he educated himself, qualified as a doctor, and offered his services to the London Missionary Society. A Presbyterian by upbringing, he could not accept strict Calvinist predestination and so preferred the undenominational L.M.S., though even at the time he doubted whether he could work under orders from anyone. A meeting with Robert Moffatt, himself a missionary of the L.M.S. and on leave from Africa, led to his choice of the "dark continent" for his future labours.

In a conventional sense Moffatt was a greater missionary than Livingstone. Another self-educated Scot of humble background and Presbyterian upbringing, Moffatt had been converted to Methodism, joined the L.M.S., and was sent to Africa at the age of 21. With his wife Mary, who joined him in 1819, he worked in the north, in the Bechuanaland area.

In 1825 the famous Kuruman mission station (about 120 miles north-west of Kimberley) was founded. Moffatt made gardens in the middle of a vast semi-desert area. He translated the Bible into Sechuana. He built a church to seat 500, though at first he seemed able to make no converts at all. He became, by force of circumstances, a pioneer explorer also. To obtain wood for his building he travelled through 700 miles of unexplored country-side. He several times visited Mzilikazi the Matabele chief. African converts were made at last. Outstations were set up. Kuruman became in time the centre of a great missionary district. Moffatt, weather-beaten, bearded, craggy, became a missionary hero. His book *Missionary Labours and Scenes in Southern Africa* was published in the 1840s and was something of a best-seller. On one occasion he drew so great a crowd to hear him speak at Exeter Hall that the building was filled twice over and the address had to be repeated.

This was the man who brought Livingstone to South Africa in 1840. The new missionary first spent some time in Cape Town where he made contact with Dr Philip, now London Missionary Society superintendent. The younger man began by being somewhat suspicious of his superior. He thought Philip an agitator and a meddler in matters strictly outside the province of the Church. But this phase did not last long. Livingstone was soon upbraiding Philip's own white congregation in Cape Town for being lukewarm in support of their minister. He caught Philip's determination to make the coloured people free.

After some weeks in Cape Town Livingstone moved to Moffatt's station at Kuruman. The Moffatts had not yet returned and Livingstone used the interval for the first of his journeys. He hoped to be able to found his own sub-station. For this purpose he needed a site which was free from malaria and was yet provided with a sufficient supply of water. In the dry, feverish region of the Kalahari this was far from easy. So Livingstone began to explore and his real vocation was born. As he travelled he lived with Africans, learning a little of their language, a little of their way of life and of the workings of their minds.

The Moffatts arrived back at Kuruman towards the end of 1843. Livingstone worked with them for a while. He married their daughter, Mary, early in 1845. But relations between Livingstone and the Moffatts were not entirely easy. Two such strong-minded men inevitably found it difficult to work together. Livingstone was a pioneer and an explorer: Moffatt, a builder and cultivator. Livingstone could never be still for long. Moffatt gave his whole life to Kuruman.

Livingstone had set up a new station at Mobatsa in 1843. He moved several times more, settling eventually at Kolobeng in the Kalahari. His journeys began to take him further and further afield. In 1849 he joined forces with big-game hunters in order to discover the exact position of Lake Ngami. In 1850 and again in 1851 he made further journeys northwards. Here Livingstone had his first direct experience of the evils of the slave trade which still flourished in Central Africa. African tribes disposed of their unwanted members, criminals, or captured enemies, by selling them to Arab slave traders. The Portuguese (who controlled a large part of the eastern coast line) were not enthusiastic about stopping the commerce in human beings. Guns and other products of more civilized economies made their way into the interior of Africa in exchange for the slaves who were smuggled out.

Livingstone's personal vocation had now really been formed. He was to be a Christian explorer. The vocation to be an *explorer* was to become more and more insistent, but the explorer was to open the continent to "Christianity and commerce". There is something peculiarly nineteenth-century about the juxtaposing of those two words, "Christianity" and "commerce", and for Livingstone they were inseparable. It was the slave trade which made them so. Christian morality demanded that the filthy buying and selling be stopped. Christianity would teach the tribes to have a proper respect for the dignity of human beings. But commerce was almost as important, in this war on slavery, as Christianity. Until they had some other source of income the tribes of the interior would be continually tempted to sell their fellow men and women. They had no other exportable goods. But if commerce could teach them to exploit the natural wealth of Africa they would have other commodities to sell and they would have the resources to feed the extra, unwanted, members of the tribe.

Nor was this bitter hatred of slavery the only factor which made Livingstone's vocation so insistent. He had first begun his travels because he wanted to find sites on which mission stations could be established. There was a sense in which all his later, more famous, journeyings were merely an extension of this. He saw himself as opening up the whole of Africa to the missionaries. He came to believe that it was not his job to give his whole life, as Moffatt was doing, to the building up of one particular mission. His special task was to open up the way for other missionaries, to map out the area, to indicate the needs, to be a trail-blazer and, if in the course of doing so, he sowed a few seeds of Christianity as he passed, this was almost incidental. In a sense he was still looking for suitable sites for missions. He was also looking for good land for Africans to settle on and cultivate. He feared that pressure of the white man's expansion from the south must drive the black man out before it. He feared that the tribes would take refuge in the barren, semi-desert areas where the white man would not be so tempted to follow them. So he searched for good, rich country in the interior, free from malaria and the tsetse fly, with water and fertile soil, with minerals and ivory, where the African tribesman could settle, develop, be enriched by Christianity and commerce, and be ready to meet the white men on equal terms.

The Boers of the Transvaal were, of course, the spear-head of the white man's advance. Livingstone believed, and said, that the Boers were slave-owners. Indentured labour and the subject condition of tribesmen in the Transvaal amounted, in his eyes, to a thinly disguised form of slavery. Somewhat naturally the Boers, in their turn, resented the charge. Their republican constitution specifically declared that slavery was not to be permitted. But it also carefully preserved the superior rights of the white man, exempted him from corporal punishment, and forbad English missionaries to work in the Transvaal. And the Trekkers in turn argued that Livingstone was a gun-runner. The arguments on both sides are complicated and the evidence obscure. In 1852 Livingstone's station at Kolobeng was attacked and destroyed during his absence in Cape Town. This may have been done by a party of Boers looking for the arms which Livingstone was said to be supplying to Africans. Or it may have been done by a band of African marauders. Livingstone's own account places the blame firmly on the Boers and says that what the raiders thought was a terrible cannon, was nothing more dangerous than a huge black cooking pot. Whether one may seriously believe that a Boer commando could make a mistake of this sort will remain a matter of personal opinion. It is clear that Livingstone gave some small gifts of arms and ammunition to chiefs whom he befriended. That he was ever a gun-runner or a deliberate fomenter of war between Boer and African is unlikely. It is, however, possible that Livingstone did not object to being labelled in this way. If rumour said he was arming the tribesmen, rumour itself might deter the Boers from making an attack on an enemy which they believed to be well armed.

After 1852 Livingstone was far more concerned with central than with southern Africa. He continued to resent the restrictions which conventional missionary work placed upon his special vocation. He eventually resigned from the London Missionary Society altogether and was employed by the Royal Geographical Society. He still believed himself to be working for the opening up of the continent for Christianity. All his explorations had this end in view, and one episode in particular illustrates how he thought his work fitted into the general pattern of African missions.

In 1857 Livingstone visited Cambridge and stirred up a great missionary enthusiasm in the university. In the following year Robert Gray, Anglican bishop of Cape Town, also visited the university. He was anxious to establish missionary work in Zululand but, finding that Livingstone had aroused so much interest in Central Africa, decided instead to channel this interest into creating a mission on the Zambesi. The Universities' Mission to Central Africa was formed. An Anglican archdeacon from Natal, Mackenzie, was made bishop to head the new mission, and Livingstone took the party out to the site of the proposed station in the heart of Africa. The mission itself was a failure. Livingstone and Mackenzie liberated a party of slaves and Mackenzie then found himself saddled with these unfortunates. To send them back to their own tribes would only mean that they would be sold all over again. Eventually there came the time when the bishop found himself fighting a minor war, rifle in hand, to liberate and protect other slaves. Under these conditions the mission could not flourish. Moreover there was considerable tension between Livingstone and Mackenzie. Their personalities were very different. Their interpretations of Christian piety were contradictory. Fever decimated the mission party. Livingstone, who was after all a doctor, had invented a pill which he called a "rouser" and which he believed to be an infallible cure for the fevers of Africa. But the pill was less effective than Livingstone had hoped. In 1862 Livingstone came back from Cape Town, with reinforcements for the mission, to find that the bishop had died and that the work, which was only a few months old, had already been abandoned.

Although the Zambesi mission was a failure it shows how

Livingstone hoped that his work might be used. He would open the path, others must settle along it. He was not interested in denominational concerns. Mackenzie's party were mostly very high Church Anglicans! Livingstone, nevertheless, really tried to help them as much as he could, in spite of the tensions and misunderstandings. By the time he died, in 1873, he had made it possible for missions to reach parts of the continent which would otherwise still have been closed to them.

9. The Origins of the "Hervormde" and "Gereformeerde" Churches

We have already seen how tenuous was the connection between the Cape Church and the Trekkers, and have noted some of the factors which would make it difficult for the connection to be re-established. But this is by no means the whole of the story. It must not be thought that the services of an ex-L.M.S. mission teacher, a Methodist, and an American, constituted the whole of the normal religious exercises of the Trekkers. We know that the Bible was one of their most treasured possessions. We know that on the whole the Trekkers were a particularly pious and devoted people. We have record of Cilliers and other leaders conducting prayers before battle. It is a matter of the most general knowledge that the original church in Pietermaritzburg was built in consequence of the vow taken before Blood River. Again and again there is evidence to suggest that the Trekkers thought of themselves as somehow like the Israelites of the Old Testament, led by God into the wilderness, beset by heathen enemies, but nevertheless being guided towards a promised land. And this idea seems to have burnt itself deeply into the imagination of the Trekkers. It was possible at last for their Volksraad (legislature) to maintain that, in attacking them, Mzilikazi had been challenging the power of God himself.

It is plain, then, that religion was something which was prominent in Trekker thought and in their way of life. To be cut off from the Cape Church and its ministers might mean that the emigrants would have to forgo the sacraments and a good many of the normal features of Christian community life. But it did not mean that they were cut off from religion. On the contrary they were living under conditions in which they were almost daily in contact with the harshest of realities, in which danger and death were always present. In such circumstances religion is likely to be a constant source of strength. They had to rely on God for there was no one else to turn to. They were living, moreover, in circumstances in which the record of God's dealings with his chosen people seemed peculiarly apt. There developed amongst them a type of piety which was simple, direct, based upon the most literal application of biblical texts to the business of daily life. Most of them were of no great education. They possessed a strong sense of the family. Their Christianity was the religion of the household. It was patriarchal rather than sacerdotal. The father of the family, the leader of each group, must provide the devotional exercises which were necessary. A man like Sarel Cilliers would preach if necessary, and it was he who administered the vow on the eve of Blood River. The patriarchal figure of the leader of each group of Trekkers became the prototype of the religious leader. He was so much more real to his followers than the distant, critical *predikant* of the colony.

For those of the emigrants who were also Doppers, like Hendrik Potgieter who eventually established his followers at Potchefstroom in the Transvaal, this kind of religion came all the more easily. They had long been suspicious of innovating parsons and the new ways of doing things. They were in any case anxious to restore a conservative, unchanging, stricter religion.

It was this difference in day-to-day piety, even more than the tensions of the first days of the Trek, which made it so difficult for the Church to resume relationships with the emigrants in the 1840s. The polished, educated *predikant*, capable of writing official letters immaculately in both Dutch and English, praying for the Queen, and talking eloquently of ritual and doctrine, must have seemed like a visitor from another world. The Cape Church had remained what it had been, the official church of the Colony, and the Trekkers had moved away from it metaphorically as well as literally. There was a whole vital phase of the lives of the people in which the official Church had not shared. The clergy had been, in the eyes of the Trekkers, like Jonahs who had successfully defied the call of God.

As the forties wore on one attempt after another was made to re-establish the connection. The Trekkers in the north appealed on several occasions for a permanent minister of their own, or at least for a visit from someone who could administer the sacraments. Again and again the attempts were bedevilled by political fears. It must be remembered that the Trekkers had emigrated because the government had tried to contain them, to hem them in with frontiers, and to take from them rights which they believed to be essential to their way of life. Over and over again the government tried to have the best of both worlds—forbidding colonists to cross the frontiers, and then annexing their new territories when they had escaped. This had happened in Natal. The Trekkers turned back across the Drakensberg. The territory between the Orange and the Vaal rivers was annexed and became the Orange River Sovereignty. It was part of the tragedy that the annexation coincided with the visit of the first commission appointed by the Cape Church to try to restore a full and formal relationship with the Trekkers. The rumour got about that the government was planning to use the Cape Church as a means of getting its hands on the Trekkers again. One of the members of the deputation caused a further stir by saying that there were those who wished to fear God *and* honour the Queen.

Unhappy incidents of this kind seem to have occurred whenever an attempt was made to reunite the Trekkers with the Cape Church. The second commission or deputation from the Cape visited the Trekker communities in the same year as the first (1848). Again there was great clumsiness associated with its appointment. One of the members was a clergyman who had described the murder of Retief as God's judgment on the Trek. And the whole work of the commission became suspect when the word got about that its expenses had been paid by the colonial administration. The third deputation went north in 1852. This time, perhaps because the younger Andrew Murray was a member, personal relations with the Trekkers were rather easier.

By this time there were four officially constituted congregations in the Transvaal. The southernmost was near Potchefstroom and the others were strung out along a line northwards. The newest was the Soutpansberg congregation, almost as far north as the banks of the Limpopo. From the point of view of these communities the crucial issue was whether they would be sent a minister. For the commission, the basic concern was whether these communities were willing to be subject to the authority of the Cape Synod, even though politically they were entirely and determinedly independent of Cape Town. The Trekkers agreed to accept Cape clergymen on these terms but it would seem that it was never clearly stated by the commission that the Cape Church was still controlled by the ordinance of 1843 which, amongst other things, reserved certain rights to the governor in the appointment of all clergymen. Another matter, which was later to become vitally important, seems to have been overlooked by everyone. The ordinance of 1843 specifically defined the Dutch Reformed Church as the Church *in the Cape Colony*.

Towards the end of 1852 when the commission had returned to the Cape, the synod met, and this very issue was raised. The attorney-general gave it as his opinion that the incorporation of the Transvaal congregations in the Cape Church would not be in conflict with the ordinance. A year or two earlier the congregations in the Orange River Sovereignty and in Natal had already been formed into a presbytery of the Cape Church.

The Transvaal congregations three times "called" ministers from the south. Each time the attempt came to nothing. Political differences amongst the Trekkers played their part in increasing the ecclesiastical unsettlement. By the so-called Sand River Convention of 1852 the British authorities promised the Transvaalers freedom to manage their own affairs. But quarrels and misunderstandings between various groups of Trekkers continued. Various little republics co-existed uneasily. Some desired ecclesiastical independence. Others favoured incorporation in the Cape Church. Feuds became hereditary. Rival constitutions for rival republics became badges of local allegiance. It was not until 1856 and 1857 that the South African republic, complete with constitution, president, and flag, took shape north of the Vaal. Even then Soutpansberg in the north and Lydenburg in the east, two areas of considerable size, remained outside it for some ten years. In the meantime the British government decided to abandon the Orange River Sovereignty which became the Trekker republic of the Orange Free State in 1854.

In November 1852 a Dutch minister, Dirk van der Hoff,

arrived at the Cape. He had been recommended to the Transvaal Volksraad (parliament) and it was intended that he should go north to the emigrant congregations. Officials of the Cape Synod advised him to take the oath of allegiance to the queen so that he could be appointed to his cure by the governor. Van der Hoff refused. When he arrived at Potchefstroom in May 1853 he was further advised to refuse to be installed by a representative of the Cape Church. Though van der Hoff was himself in favour of union with the Cape Church, the general feeling was against. Hymn-singing became an issue once more. The general conservatism of the Trekkers, and particularly of the Doppers, and their political fears and suspicions were too strong.

Van der Hoff, whatever his personal opinion might be, was willing to abide by the general decision. The *Hervormde Kerk*, as the Transvaal Church was called, became an entirely separate and independent body. It is fair, to represent it at first, and in practice, as the "Dutch Reformed Church in the Transvaal".[1] There would appear to have been no intention to separate from communion with the Cape Church. What was rejected was an organic union. It is only in later history that real schism developed and there was a *Nederduitse Gereformeerde Kerk* and a *Hervormde Kerk* side by side in the Transvaal. The *Hervormde Kerk* meanwhile became by stages the established Church of the republic. The constitution of 1856 recognized it formally and at the same time specifically declared that there was to be no equality of black and white in either Church or State. In 1856 the independence of the *Hervormde Kerk* from the Cape Church was plainly asserted and in 1860 it was made the official State Church of the Republic. In 1862 the general assembly of the Church agreed on a Church order which became law in the following year.

[1] I am using "Dutch Reformed Church" as the equivalent of Nederduitse Gereformeerde Kerk—i.e. the Cape Church and its sister Churches. These were, until recently, only very loosely federated but are now more closely united and may properly be described as a single Church. "Hervormde" means "re-formed"; "gereformeerde" means "reformed". But it would be pedantic to keep using these words in English and I shall use the names "Hervormde" and "Gereformeerde" for the two Afrikaner Churches, which are quite distinct from the "Dutch Reformed Church" proper.

But in matters such as the appointment of the clergy the State connection was very much looser than that in the Cape.

It was not long before the new establishment was challenged. In Holland the Dutch Reformed Church in the nineteenth century was itself split by schisms. Erastianism, the right of Christians to secede from the State Church, and the bitterness provoked by rationalism and theological liberalism were all thorny issues. The prevalent liberalism and the protection afforded to it by the State connection was condemned by Willem Bilderdijk. Conservatism was taken further by his followers who began, like the Doppers in South Africa, to criticize the use of hymns in worship. Eventually in 1839 a Christian Reformed Church was created, an independent, unestablished body which claimed, nevertheless, to have remained true to the decisions of the Synod of Dort. A strongly evangelical and perhaps pietistic strain seems to have been a feature of its pattern of life and worship.

A minister of this persuasion, Ds D. Postma, came to the Transvaal in 1858. Postma was intended to be a sort of ecclesiastical prospector whose job was to investigate conditions in the Transvaal and decide whether the Christian Reformed Church could help in any way, either by undertaking missionary work or by providing clergy for unshepherded congregations. While he was still in the Cape he was on the friendliest of terms with the clergy there and was recognized as an ordained minister, being invited to take services and to preach. On his way to the north he was approached by emissaries of the Rustenburg congregation in the Transvaal and invited to become their minister. When he arrived he discovered that the congregation there was bitterly divided over the thorny question of hymn-singing. At a general Church meeting at Potchefstroom in December 1858 Postma and van der Hoff seemed to be on the friendliest terms. It is true that one of the Rustenburg delegates moved for the banning of hymns, but the matter was deferred. In the following month van der Hoff presided at a meeting at Rustenburg at which the issue was again discussed and tempers got out of control, but because a general meeting was planned for later in the same month a final decision was again postponed. In Pretoria on 10 January 1859 delegates from Potchefstroom, Soutpansberg, Rustenburg, and Pretoria assembled to settle the matter. Postma was asked to explain his mission and to assert his orthodoxy. This he did. He was then asked his opinion of hymn-singing. His reply was that hymns of which the words were not taken from the Bible were better left out since they might split the Church. The outcome of the proceedings was that Postma was declared to be acceptable to the Transvaal Church but that clergymen of the Christian Reformed Church might be *required* to use hymns in public worship. Van der Hoff had made every possible attempt at compromise but the assembly insisted on the legitimacy of hymn-singing and, in consequence, the Dopper element broke away to form the *Gereformeerde Kerk*.

Van der Hoff and the *Hervormde Kerk* were regarded by this party as far too liberal, though in comparison with the Cape Church they were extremely conservative. Fifteen leading dissidents assembled on the same day as the decision was taken by the assembly and declared that they had ceased to be members of the State Church. They gave notice of their intention to form a free Church which would adhere to the standards of faith, order, and morals laid down by the synod of Dort. The Rustenburgers were, of course, the core of this body. Amongst them was Paul Kruger, a rising politician, who was eventually to become the great president and hero of the republic. All over the Transvaal small groups of Doppers came out in favour of an independent, separated Church, and even south of the Vaal the movement gained some support. Denominationalism had become a fact. But in spite of the failure of all attempts to restore unity it would appear that Postma and van der Hoff maintained friendly personal relations. Indeed, there was probably less bitterness after the separation than before it.

10. Bishop Colenso[1]

John William Colenso was born in 1814. At Cambridge he gained a reputation as a brilliant mathematician. He taught for a while at Harrow and then married and was appointed to a parish in Norfolk. Here he began to take an interest in missionary matters and when Bishop Gray was looking for a man to become first bishop of the new diocese of Natal, Colenso was recommended to him.

By the time Colenso became bishop of Natal in 1853 his theology, such as it was, was already developed. With his mathematical training and his scientific interests he was on the side of the rationalists. Like most of the early Liberal Protestants he had something to say which was fresh and original as compared with the stuffy dogmatism of orthodoxy. He protested against the "hell-fire" preaching of most missionaries of his age, who presented the heathen with a clear choice between conversion and a graphically described perdition. He refused to accept that every custom of the heathen must be evil, just because it *was* their custom. He placed his confidence in the natural goodness of man and the reliability of human reason.

The new bishop came to his diocese in January 1854 and spent three months making a preliminary tour before returning to England to try to find men and money for the work. As part of his campaign he published the journal of his visitation—*Ten Weeks in Natal*—and was at once in the thick of bitter controversy. The real issue was how far can the Christian gospel be communicated by people of one culture to people of another.

[1] The substance of this chapter first appeared in the *Journal of Ecclesiastical History*, Vol. XIII, No. 2.

Victorian missionaries in South Africa inclined to the view that British civilization and Christianity were almost identical. They thought of African culture as heathen, the work of the devil, to be rooted out as soon as possible. But Colenso argued that the savage was noble and that the missionary ought to attempt to build upon the element of nobility in African religion.

Other missionaries objected most of all to the fact that Colenso allowed polygamists to be baptized. The bishop was by no means in favour of polygamy as such, but he maintained that it was part of the Zulu social order, and that it was not necessarily immoral. He thought it most certainly *was* immoral to make converts put away their extra wives. He believed that polygamists should be baptized, but that men who were already Christians should not be allowed to marry more than once. The controversy which followed lasted some years and produced a spate of pamphlets. Missionary opinion was overwhelmingly against him. In the end his policy failed, too, for some of his young men relapsed into polygamy. They simply could not see why they should be refused a second wife because they happened to have been "born" Christians.

Meanwhile Colenso was in trouble with the settler laity of Durban. He was accused of being a papist in disguise because he insisted on the use of the surplice, the "offertory" (collection), and the Prayer for the Church Militant. A "Church of England Defence Association" was formed to resist these popish ways. The bishop was burnt in effigy in the Durban market square. And at that point he gave way to popular opinion.

Colenso was in process of organizing his diocese. He planned to have a single, central, well-manned centre of missionary operations just outside Pietermaritzburg, so that he could supervise work amongst both white settlers and Africans. The mission station was to contain a school, a theological college, farms, a church, and a printing press. By 1861 Colenso had spent over £11,000 on the station. From this centre he sought to reach the Zulu nation as a whole. He sought to Christianize a whole culture and society, rather than to make members of that society conform to the patterns of Christian living. He formed a close association with Theophilus Shepstone, Natal's secretary for Native Affairs, whose policy was to strengthen tribal structure and native laws and gradually to substitute the authority of the colonial administration for that of the chiefs.

But Colenso was at loggerheads with his clergy. In 1856 he appointed James Green, the priest at Pietermaritzburg, to be dean of the cathedral. In 1858 the bishop preached a series of sermons in the cathedral in which he maintained that Christ was present in the eucharist in exactly the same way as at other times. The sacrament itself, he held, was little more than an aid to devotion. Green objected violently, virtually maintaining that transubstantiation was the only orthodox view. He accused Colenso of heresy and reported the matter to Bishop Gray. Gray was in England at the time and he refused to take any action.

But if Gray thought he could shrug off the Colenso controversy so easily he was greatly mistaken. The situation was made more tense by the publication in 1861 of Colenso's *St Paul's Epistle to the Romans: newly translated and explained from a missionary point of view*. This book was based on lectures given by the bishop to a party of workers he had brought out to Natal in 1856. It was in a very real sense an attempt to set out the *essentials* of the gospel in relation to the very book in the New Testament normally regarded as enshrining the doctrine of justification by faith. Colenso attacked penal substitution, denying not only that Christ had died to placate an angry Father, but also that God has any righteous anger against sin at all. He held that all men are justified in Christ from their very birth hour; baptism is merely a recognition and proclamation of this fact. The gospel is preached to the heathen, not to convert him but to set before him a pattern of love so that he may follow it.

Bishop Gray tried to persuade Colenso to withdraw the book. When he refused, Gray referred the matter to the Archbishop of Canterbury. Gray and Colenso both went to England to await the archbishop's decision. But the archbishop died before any action had been taken. At that point Colenso published the first part of a critical work on the Old Testament—*The Pentateuch and the Book of Joshua Critically Examined*.

Questions asked by Zulu converts had made Colenso doubt whether the Old Testament was really superior to African folktales. The bad arithmetic of the Old Testament convinced him that it could not be verbally inerrant. And it seems as though Colenso could find no half-way position. If the Bible was not literally the words of God then it was no more inspired than were the works of "Cicero, Lactantius, and the Sikh Gooroos".

Publication at this moment was a tragedy. A great many people condemned the bishop of Natal for the wrong reason. Archbishop Longley of Canterbury gathered together a collection of English, Irish, and colonial bishops who agreed to inhibit Colenso in their dioceses. The doctrine of the atonement, which was the real point at issue, was forgotten in a rising wave of hysteria about "biblical criticism". Colenso's naive and negative, but quite useful, scholarship was made into a whip to beat him with.

Colenso was formally delated for heresy by three clergymen, and Gray cited him to appear before his court in November 1863. The court consisted of the other three South African bishops and it found Colenso guilty on all nine charges brought against him. Colenso was not present, but was represented by Dr W. Bleek, curator of the public library in Cape Town, and one of the earliest anthropologists in South Africa. He was the son of Friedrich Bleek, a German biblical scholar, whose work had influenced Colenso considerably.

Of the nine charges against Colenso, three revealed errors in his opponents' theology as much as in his own; two quite rightly accused him of preaching a universalist gospel; two were really concerned with biblical criticism; and two attacked his theology of the atonement and the sacraments. Colenso regarded the court of the South African bishops as a travesty of British justice. The Crown was the one arbiter whom he trusted to guarantee the religious liberty of Her Majesty's subjects. He petitioned the Queen-in-Council direct. Gray wrote him one last letter, begging him to recant, but the letter was not perhaps very tactfully worded for the purpose. Colenso was unmoved by it. Gray issued a sentence of excommunication, took charge of the diocese of Natal, and began to take steps to find a new bishop. Colenso remained in England until the judgment of the Privy Council was known.

The judgment was not delivered until March 1865. The judicial committee held that, though the Crown could create ecclesiastical persons, it could not give them jurisdiction in colonies which possessed their own legislatures. Gray could exercise no authority over Colenso. Almost by accident the Anglican Church in South Africa discovered that it was not established.

Colenso returned to Natal in the latter part of 1865. He frankly attempted to appeal to the sentiment of the colonial laity by claiming to be discharging "the duties committed to me by the Queen". He sued the Colonial Bishoprics Fund for his salary and won the suit. The Natal courts gave him possession of all Church property in the colony except for one mission station in the south.

On the other hand Gray and the orthodox party received modified support from the convocation of Canterbury and from the Lambeth Conference. Neither body would declare Colenso excommunicate, but both agreed that Gray might appoint a new bishop for Natal, and after a long search he was able to persuade an English clergyman, W. K. Macrorie, to accept the bishopric in January 1867. When the dust had died down a bit and it was possible to make any sort of assessment of the position in Natal, the state of the parties was seen to be fairly evenly balanced with a slight advantage to the orthodox. All the clergy save three accepted the new bishop. But the orthodox party lost all its property except one mission station. The laity were about evenly divided—which created an awkward social situation for those who regarded themselves as being " C. of E. " Sir Garnet Wolseley is said, as governor of Natal, to have handled the unpleasanter social consequences of the schism by inviting both bishops to dinner, but attending neither of their cathedrals.

But time was all on the side of the orthodox. Colenso could find few suitable clergymen. Time after time the priests whom he licensed turned out to be scandalous or rogues. But curiously it is at this point in his history, when apparently everything is seedy and down-at-heel, that Colenso comes into his own. The bishop could no longer care for his considerable following of Africans, because he lacked the men and the money to run his missions properly, but he devoted the greater part of his last years to securing justice for the African people in a colony where the

6

"native policy" was notoriously illiberal even for South Africa. And his crusade was the more courageous because it cost him the friendship of his most influential lay supporter, Sir Theophilus Shepstone.

Colenso had always been an advocate of political and social justice, encouraging Africans to make full use of such political rights as the law allowed them. His first major skirmish with the colonial authorities was on behalf of Langalibalele, a chief arrested in 1873 for refusing to obey an order to disarm his tribe. He was tried in a court which Colenso believed to be prejudiced and unfair. Langalibalele was sentenced to death, but the sentence was commuted to one of banishment. Throughout the proceedings, and in the face of violent public hostility, Colenso did everything to secure fair treatment for the accused. It is to be feared that the orthodox rejoiced at his growing unpopularity. Yet, almost single-handed, he achieved some success. Langalibalele was moved to a pleasanter place of exile, and the bishop's protests in England were partly responsible for the retirement of the governor of Natal.

The Langalibalele trial had certain important consequences in that it re-opened the case of another chief, Matyana, though it was already twenty years old. The details of Matyana's offence do not matter. The real point at issue was that Matyana alleged that he had been treacherously dealt with by Shepstone's brother, John. Colenso insisted that the whole Matyana incident be investigated in spite of being threatened with a libel action. A government court of inquiry was appointed and found against John Shepstone, though it attempted to minimize the blame to be attached to him.

So much criticism of the Natal administration led to an attempt at reform in the colony, but it also led to a personal rivalry between Shepstone and Colenso. Shepstone wished to be given full powers to govern the African people, and he would no doubt have exercised those powers in a fatherly, if autocratic, manner. Colenso proposed that he should himself be made the official "protector" of the Zulu nation. Neither gained what he asked for. A native affairs commission was appointed to govern the tribes.

The fourth and final episode in Colenso's crusade concerned

the treatment meted out to the Zulu king, Cetshwayo, after the Zulu war of 1878 and 1879. Cetshwayo was captured and his territory divided amongst thirteen petty chiefs. The king himself was imprisoned in Cape Town. Colenso, in alliance with F. W. Chesson, secretary of the Aboriginees Protection Society, began a new campaign against the Natal administration. In particular the bishop claimed that Cetshwayo had been incited to make war so that he could be removed. Colenso's printing press on his mission station turned out pamphlet after pamphlet. He helped Cetshwayo obtain permission to go to England where he was received by the Queen, but before the affair was finally settled Colenso was dead. He died on 20 June 1883.

There can be no doubt of the impact of Colenso's life on South African Anglicanism. He had introduced biblical criticism into the sub-continent. He had advocated revolutionary and unpopular missionary policies. He had been responsible, in spite of himself, for the existence of an autonomous Anglican province organized on a voluntary basis. And he had asserted very firmly that the Christian gospel possessed definite social implications.

11. *Missionary Conflict and Growth in the North*

Competition to "sell" rival brands of the Christian faith was the great curse of nineteenth century missionary expansion, but it did not really make itself felt in South Africa until after 1850. It is true that L.M.S. missionaries wrote home complaining of Methodist "intrusion" and "aggression". Methodists likewise complained about the setting up of "Church" (i.e. Anglican) missions. But there was so much room, so many heathen, and so few missionaries that these grumbles were not terribly important.

In the Cape Colony itself, by 1850, the Moravians had their village settlements for the Cape Coloured folk in the western districts and other denominations, such as the Methodists, the Anglicans, and the Rhenish Mission were beginning work there too. Further north both the L.M.S. and the Methodists had established stations. In Namaqualand Barnabas Shaw's pioneering work had led to the creation of permanent and growing missions amongst the Hottentots and Africans. The Methodists had, indeed, tried to penetrate even further into the desert regions of what is now South-West Africa and their letters and journals make fictional adventure stories seem tame in the extreme. But these remoter missions were difficult to maintain. Both the L.M.S. stations in Namaqualand and the Methodist ones further north were eventually handed over, not without some unhappiness, to the Rhenish Society which had been founded in 1828. The Rhenish missionaries settled first in the Western Cape and, by 1840, had penetrated into Namaqualand. Ten years later they had established a virtual monopoly in this area and by painstaking and patient work had built up small Christian communities settled in cultivated oases in the desert.

Further east, in Bechuanaland, the L.M.S. had mission stations serving the Griqua people and the African tribes. This was the region in which Moffatt was the giant and where his station at Kuruman was now a thriving centre of every kind of missionary activity. Other attempts, like Lindley's, to set up missions in this area had been ephemeral, but further east again the missionary scene was more crowded. The Berlin Missionary Society had sent five missionaries to South Africa in 1834 and two stations had been established amongst the Hottentots in what was to become the Orange Free State. The Methodist missionary E. Edwards, originally an assistant to Barnabas Shaw, had set up a mission with the Barolong at Thaba 'Nchu and this had become a thriving centre for Methodist operations among African tribes, disturbed and scattered by the expansion of the Zulu empire in the east.

In the same central area Moshesh created his kingdom of Basutoland, a core of Southern-Sotho people with an admixture of other African refugees. Moshesh's great ability and the strong strategic situation of his kingdom made it one of the most important features of the South African scene in the second and third quarters of the century. Here the Paris Evangelical Missionary Society was the pioneer body. The first French missionaries arrived in 1829. One of them settled in the Western Cape but the rest went north to work amongst a tribe that was subject to Mzilikazi. The attempt failed but in 1833, under Eugéne Casalis, the society began work in Basutoland. Until Roman Catholic missionaries arrived in Basutoland in the 1850s this was P.E.M.S. territory.

In Natal the American Board, with which Lindley was associated, was the oldest and strongest body at work, but the Methodists and the Berlin Society also had their stations there. The Norwegian Missionary Society had begun work in Zululand in 1844 and the Anglicans, under Colenso, were also to appear in this eastern area soon after 1850. South of Natal there were the mission stations of the L.M.S. and the Methodists, which have already been dealt with in earlier chapters. There were Scottish missionaries there, too, and beginnings of Anglican work.

Missionary expansion after 1850 brought conflict and competition and it was often, but not always, the arrival of Anglican missionaries which sparked it off. The first Anglican bishop in South

Africa, Robert Gray, was appointed in 1848. He found very little
Anglican work of any kind and virtually no missions. In order to
make it possible for the work to be done effectively he was determined to subdivide his huge diocese. Anglican missions then
began to appear in the Eastern Cape and Natal. But Gray was far
from content. We have seen how he utilized the missionary
enthusiasm, awakened by Livingstone at Cambridge, to launch
the Zambezi venture. From this time onwards Gray was abso-
lutely convinced that there was only one way to plan a mission
satisfactorily—mark out an area (adjacent to an already established diocese), constitute it a missionary diocese, and send in a
team of missionaries led by a bishop from the very start. Such a
markedly geographical concept of missionary strategy was bound
to lead to conflict. Other missionaries might well resent finding
themselves one morning within the boundaries of an Anglican
diocese. Moreover Gray was much in sympathy with the Tractarian or Oxford Movement. Men like Keble, Newman, and
Pusey had re-awakened in the Church of England an awareness
of things "catholic". Gray, though not strictly a Tractarian,
agreed with their "high" doctrine of the Church, the ministry,
and the sacraments. And the long Colenso controversy had the
effect of attracting English Tractarians to South Africa where the
true faith seemed to be so heroically defended against the notorious heretic. Such men, when they reached South Africa, would
not find it easy to treat Calvinist, Methodist, or L.M.S. missionaries as representatives of the one, holy, catholic, and apostolic
Church.

Basutoland was the scene of one of the resulting conflicts.
Moshesh had been asking for an English bishop, perhaps because
he thought it would be politic for him to own one of Queen
Victoria's religious experts. In 1863 Edward Twells, a staunch
Tractarian, was made bishop of an area including Basutoland and
the Orange Free State. On his way to Bloemfontein, his see city,
he visited Moshesh and Moroka (the Barolong chief) making it
plain that he planned to send missions to both. The Methodist
and P.E.M.S. missionaries, who had been established in this area
for thirty years, protested at once; but Twells persisted nor did
his departure solve the problem.

There was also a good deal of conflict in the Transvaal, though it came later there because missions were slow in developing in the north. The Trekkers were ill-disposed, as we have seen, to English missionaries. Moreover there was, at one time, a schism within the *Gereformeerde Kerk* over whether it was theologically right to undertake missionary work amongst Africans at all.[1] The view that it was not right was, however, a somewhat "lunatic fringe" opinion. The majority were convinced that missions were right and proper but did not see how it was possible to do the job when clergymen could not even be found for all the "white" congregations. The Cape Church managed to set up two or three missions in the Transvaal in the late 1850s, importing missionaries from Europe for the purpose. In 1860 the Berlin Society sent two men to the north, first to Swaziland where they met with little success, and then on into the Transvaal. Here they settled, with the permission of the Boers, and though their first station had to be abandoned the Berlin missionaries eventually created a strong network in Sekukuniland and have always been one of the largest missionary bodies in the Transvaal.

Methodists and Anglicans, representing "English" Christianity, arrived in the Transvaal at much the same time. English political interest was moving north too. In 1867 diamonds were discovered on the northern fringes of the Cape, where the frontiers were vague and disputed and no one was certain whether the land was British, Boer, or Griqua territory. By 1871, after the Keate Award, Britain had acquired possession of the diamond fields. Southern Africa was being dragged into a new age of international finance, of cities, industries, railways, and technology. The Cape was given responsible government in 1872. The idea of a federation was revived. In 1874 Benjamin Disraeli, Britain's prime minister, appointed Lord Carnarvon to be secretary of state for the colonies and Carnarvon was anxious to persuade the "white" South African states to agree to federation. In the Transvaal there was by this time one single republic, but southern Africa was still a "balkan" jigsaw of political units of every imaginable kind.

[1] A. D. Pont, "'n Ontleding van die Teologiese-dogmatiese agtergrond van Ds. S. D. Venter se Afskeiding van die Gereformeerde Kerk in die O.V.S.", *Hervormde Teologiese Studies*, Vol. XVI, pp. 89f.

Boer suspicion of British imperialism was by no means allayed by talk of federation. The "native problem" still largely consisted of keeping powerful and more or less independent African chiefs from attacking the frontiers of the Boer republics and the British colonies.

At this stage both the Anglicans and the Methodists began making unofficial and exploratory probes into the Transvaal. A Methodist minister called Blencowe, who was stationed in Natal, visited the northern republic briefly in 1871. Two years later he was back again, this time officially, to set up a "trial mission" with three companions. One of these, George Weavind, was to become extremely important in the history of Methodism in the Transvaal. In the same year the Anglican bishop of Zululand, T. E. Wilkinson, crossed the border into the republic on an unofficial visit of reconnaissance.

The Methodists and Anglicans were alike in possessing scattered white adherents in the republic. The Germans of the Berlin Mission were concerned only with Africans, but Wilkinson and Blencowe were also following up their own folks. Plans were interrupted by political events. The Bapedi chief, Sekukuni, who had done everything in his power to prevent the Berlin missionaries from working amongst his people, attacked the Transvaal republic. Sir Theophilus Shepstone, architect of the Natal native policy, acted under the shelter of Carnarvon's federation plans and annexed the Transvaal in 1877. It was argued that annexation was necessary to prevent a general outbreak of native wars throughout the sub-continent. In fact the wars were not averted. Both the Eastern Cape and the colony of Natal passed through some dangerous times; but the Transvaal had become British territory. The English Churches began to organize themselves. The Transvaal became an Anglican diocese in 1879 and Henry Bousfield, who had already once declined to become bishop in a foreign republic, was consecrated to the new see. In 1880 the Transvaal was made a district of the Methodist Church, directly under the control of the British Conference, with Owen Watkins as its first chairman.

The annexation lasted only a brief while. Both ecclesiastical leaders arrived to find a situation different from that which had obtained at the time of their appointment. Bousfield reached the Transvaal only to land in the thick of a Boer revolt which led to the retrocession of the territory by Britain. Watkins' arrival was similarly delayed by the war and he was unable to take up his new office till 1881.

The two men, whose coming to the Transvaal has something of the appearance of a race, were very different in character. Watkins was earnest, imaginative, less concerned with the Transvaal as an end in itself than with its potentialities as a base for missionary expansion northwards into Mashonaland, in what is now Rhodesia. Bousfield was a stickler for legal forms and ceremonies, not uninterested in missions but basically pessimistic about the future of Anglicanism in what was once again a republic. The atmosphere of competition remained and Bousfield's tactlessness did nothing to dispel it. On one occasion he visited a little country town where there was as yet no Anglican church. He was lent the home of a Methodist in which to hold his service and took the opportunity to preach against the pretensions of Methodism!

Bousfield's deep pessimism and his difficult temperament, which put him on bad terms with his own clergy as well as with Methodists, made it almost impossible for him to plan imaginatively for expansion. But the Methodists under Watkins had, by 1883, developed a farsighted strategy for a three-pronged drive to the north. This was, in a sense, an elaboration of the sort of chain of missions created by William Shaw. There were to be three chains—one based on Bechuanaland, one on the Transvaal, and one on Swaziland—and their objective would be Mashonaland. The work went ahead rapidly. Extensive use was made of Africans as lay preachers, assistant missionaries and, eventually, as full ministers and outstanding results were achieved.

This Methodist expansion did not go unobserved. Bousfield was not the only objector. A German missionary called Winter protested to Watkins against expansion into Sekukuniland and in 1885 the Methodist synod debated a suggestion made by the Berlin Mission that each body confine itself to a defined area. The synod refused to be bound by such an agreement and again the problem was shelved. What finally halted the outward drive of

Methodist missions was the discovery of gold on the Witwaters-rand in 1886. The rapid growth of the new mining industry created a new missionary problem. African labour, from a great many tribes and speaking different languages, flocked to the mines and were housed in rudimentary compounds. This was a mission field quite different from the old pattern where missionaries had dealt with one tribe, living still in its traditional, rural, tribalized society. Bousfield could not be convinced that gold-mining had come to stay. Only an open and scandalous controversy between the bishop and his clergy prevented him from withdrawing Anglicans from the gold fields altogether. At the same time Methodist energies were being diverted from the north to the Witwatersrand itself. Watkins retired in 1891 and was succeeded as chairman by George Weavind who developed a new and vigorous mission centred on Johannesburg.

The Anglo-Boer war broke out in 1899, after a long period of growing tension in which the discovery of gold played no small part. Bousfield had never been on good terms with the republican government. He was too English and too much the prelate. He and his clergy either fled or were sent out of the country when the war started. Weavind, on the other hand, had always been on good terms with the Boers. His brother-in-law was an important official in the republican government. It is true that Blencowe was less friendly to the Transvaal authorities and there were several occasions on which Methodists criticized the government. But on the whole Methodist ministers were able to advise their people to shoulder their responsibilities as citizens of the republic and to fight for it if necessary. Bousfield died before the war ended. Anglican work in the Transvaal was in ruins. But the Methodist and Berlin missions remained and were in a position to continue to expand.

12. *Andrew Murray and the Struggle between Liberals and Conservatives in the Dutch Reformed Church*

When the British administration found it difficult to fill vacancies in the ranks of the Dutch Reformed ministry at the Cape, one of the expedients they adopted was to encourage Presbyterian clergymen from Scotland to accept appointments in the colony. Dr George Thom, who had once been in charge of L.M.S. work in South Africa and had subsequently been appointed himself to take charge of the Dutch congregation at Caledon, was asked by the governor to visit Scotland and find suitable men for the Cape Church. As a result of his efforts a number of ministers came out to the colony, among them Andrew Murray who took charge of the congregation at Graaff Reinet in July 1822 and remained there for forty-five years. His son, also called Andrew, was to be one of the outstanding figures in the history of the Dutch Church at the Cape.

The younger Andrew Murray, born in 1828, was sent with his brother John to be educated in Scotland. There he became involved in Scottish Church affairs. A controversy between Moderates and the strict Calvinist Evangelicals led to a secession in 1843 when the Free Church of Scotland was formed, independent of the state and void of endowments. Since the controversy was largely concerned with the question of establishment Andrew Murray, who was much attracted by the men of the stricter persuasion, also began to consider the constitutional position of the Cape Church. Subsequently the brothers studied divinity in Holland where the Church had also been much disturbed by the rise of rationalistic theology and a controversy over Erastianism. Once more the Murrays aligned themselves with the conservative, "orthodox", and anti-Erastian party.

After ordination at the Hague in 1848 Andrew Murray returned to South Africa and was appointed minister at Bloemfontein. The Orange River Sovereignty had just been annexed and was for a brief period to be British territory. Murray was appointed to his charge by the governor of the Cape, in the normal manner of the Cape Church, and found himself with a vast area to care for—something like 50,000 square miles. His flock was relatively small, scattered on farms and in villages throughout the Sovereignty. He was received with suspicion, since he was regarded as an emissary of the British government. This suspicion he largely managed to overcome though, in one sense, it was to haunt him all his life. As an evangelical with Scots ancestry he was to be accused of watering down the Calvinism of the Reformed Church and of Anglicizing the traditions of the Boers. Yet the experience he gained in overcoming opposition of this kind was immensely helpful to him in his dealings, already mentioned, with the congregations in the Transvaal. He was so successful in winning the confidence of his prickly flock that he became their mouthpiece in negotiations with the British administration.

In 1860 Andrew Murray moved to Worcester in the Western Cape. His ministry here was marked by a quite astonishing revival movement on the evangelical pattern. Its extent and effect may perhaps best be measured by the fact that 50 young men offered themselves for the ministry. The number of persons, generally, who claimed to have passed through a conversion experience was enormous. It was something like the American "Great Awakening". The Dutch Reformed Church in the colony, perhaps even Murray himself, was quite unprepared for anything of this kind. In 1859 a theological seminary had been founded at Stellenbosch, in an attempt to overcome the very grave shortage of Reformed clergymen, so that there was some means of dealing with the new ordination candidates. What was more important, and perhaps more difficult, was to provide some means of maintaining new converts in the day to day business of Christian living. For these Murray wrote a devotional manual, *Blijf in Jezus* (in the English translation *Abide in Christ*). This was a simple, rather old-fashioned book. Christ's blood shed for sinners was Murray's favourite theme. But the work became a classic of its kind and was translated into several languages.

The revival movement spread over the whole country. In 1876 the synod appointed a committee for special evangelical preaching and Murray was a member of it. Nor was the revival confined to the established "white" congregations. Interest in missions to the heathen had been re-awakened and we have already seen how the Cape Church had assumed responsibility for missionary work in the Transvaal. Murray had been a member of the synodical committee on missions since 1857. In the 1870s he was also largely instrumental in the founding of the Wellington Missionary Training Institute. There was a great revival of enthusiasm for missionary work generally. Dutch Reformed missions spread as far afield as central and east Africa. In the rather staid and somnolent Cape Church itself there was a new spirit. Murray urged the "duty and privilege of entire consecration". A new devotion and piety of a conservative, Calvinist, and fundamentalist sort developed. The period between Ascension Day and Pentecost was made a special annual season of self-examination and spiritual advance, comparable with the observance of Lent in other traditions. And in 1880 Murray founded a society to encourage systematic prayer, Bible reading, and meditation.

Murray was not the only man whose inspiration and energy created this astonishing revival. A large number of other ministers and laymen played their part. But there is no doubt that Murray was one of the greatest, perhaps *the* greatest, figure in the Cape Church at the time, and that in almost every way he stood for and summed up the principal influences at work in the Church. In 1862 he had become moderator for the first of seven times and, as a result, found himself deeply involved in a doctrinal controversy which was almost exactly the Dutch Reformed Church equivalent of the Anglican crisis over Bishop Colenso. The same issues, Erastianism and so-called liberal theology, were the central matters in dispute. By temperament and background Murray would, in any case, have held strong views on the matter. Because he was moderator when the controversy first came to a head he became, in a sense, the leader of the conservative and "orthodox" party. What he had seen in Scotland and Holland in his youth seemed to be reappearing in South Africa.

The Cape Church, already anxious about the spread of heresy, had imposed a test of orthodoxy upon all ministers imported from abroad. In spite of the test some of the theological liberals found their way into the pulpits of the colony. At the same time conservative clergymen also were being recruited in Scotland and Switzerland where there had also been revival movements. Tension between the two elements became more and more sharp.

In 1862, at the synod at which Andrew Murray presided for the first time, a clergyman called Loedolff challenged the right of delegates from congregations beyond the frontiers of the Cape Colony itself to sit in the synod. While the synod proceeded with its business the supreme court of the colony hurriedly considered the case. The colonial ordinance of 1843, while it made the Dutch Reformed Church much more independent of the government, had defined it as the Church *in the colony*. The courts therefore found that delegates from outside the colony had no right to be members of the synod. Not only did this mean that the validity of many synodical decisions might be called in question, it also meant that the conservative group would be considerably weakened since the extra-colonial representatives belonged, on the whole, to this school of thought. Moreover there was a great deal of resentment aroused by the fact that civil legislation and the civil courts seemed to be limiting the right of the Church to guard the purity of its own doctrine.

Feeling was further exacerbated by the case of Ds Kotzé of Darling who declared himself unable to accept some of the teaching of the Church catechism on sin and evil. The synod of 1863 deposed Kotzé by a very narrow majority. Litigation again followed and the civil courts declared that the synod had no authority to depose Kotzé, since it was not acting in accordance with its own rules and since there was nothing which made it illegal for Kotzé to dissent from the catechism. Kotzé was therefore reinstated by the civil courts over the head of the synod. The conservatives protested vigorously and bitterly. Andrew Murray was deeply involved in the whole affair, both personally and in his official capacity.

In the meantime another heresy case was brewing. Ds T. F. Burgers (later to become president of the Transvaal Republic) was accused of holding unorthodox opinions about the existence of a personal devil, the sinlessness of Christ's human nature, and the resurrection and personal survival of the dead. In 1864 he was suspended from his pastoral office. After a long series of court cases the Judicial Committee of the Privy Council, as the final court of appeal for the colonies, upheld and reinstated Burgers. There was once more an outcry against Erastianism.

One of the curious by-products of the controversy was the suggestion, made about 1870, for a union between the Anglican and Dutch Reformed Churches in the colony. A pamphlet was printed outlining the suggestion. Some correspondence took place between the moderator of the Cape synod and Bishop Robert Gray. Both Churches had suffered from the ravages of liberal heresies and from the State connection. It might be possible for them to solve their problems jointly. The wide differences of theology, tradition, and Church order prevented the suggestion from ever being seriously entertained, but it is hardly possible to prevent oneself wondering what startling developments in both ecclesiastical and political history might not have followed from such a union!

In spite of the fact that at one time liberalism and conservatism had been so equally balanced in the Dutch Reformed synod, liberalism very quickly declined after the Burgers case. There were many reasons for this. The formation of a Unitarian body called the Free Protestant Church meant that the radicals tended to gravitate in that direction. The odium of the word "heresy" and resentment against an "English" government whose laws made it possible for such heresy to survive, also played their part. But probably the most important factor of all was the development of the seminary at Stellenbosch. A strong ministry was built up, obviating the need to import clergymen from abroad. And the seminary produced men who had been solidly and thoroughly trained in a conservative and "orthodox" theology that was both Calvinist and fundamentalist. By 1870 the liberals were already a rapidly dwindling group and they very soon became a tiny minority which had ceased to count.

It must be noted, finally, that the Cape Church had become, in ethos and outlook, much more like the Churches of the Boers in the north. The influence of men like Andrew Murray and the triumph of conservative theology had meant that a simple, fervent, old-fashioned piety, quite different from the usual trends that developed in most Christian Churches in the nineteenth century, had become the norm in the Cape Church. The typical clergyman was no longer the polished, elegant, perhaps rather worldly, man who had thought the Trekkers foolish, irresponsible, and anarchistic. Their place had been taken by earnest, evangelical, and conservative men of undoubted orthodoxy, identified with the Afrikaner traditions and culture.

13. Scottish Missions and Education

Since the sixteenth century the reformed Church of Scotland had been deeply concerned with education. The *Scottish Book of Discipline*, which (like the rest of the reformation of 1559/60) owed so much to Genevan inspiration, contained provision for the establishment of primary, secondary, and university education in connection with the reformed Church. Lack of financial resources among other factors made this plan impracticable, but education remained one of the great interests of the Scottish Church.

As soon as missionary enterprise became significant Scotsmen became associated with it. So Thomas Love, a graduate of Glasgow and a Presbyterian minister in London, was one of the founders of the London Missionary Society. In 1800 Love moved back to Scotland and eventually became secretary of the Glasgow Missionary Society. In 1820 Dr George Thom persuaded the society to send out a missionary to work amongst Africans in the eastern frontier region. William Thomson, who was to be employed at a salary of £100 per annum paid by the government, arrived at the Cape in company with another young Scot, John Bennie, in 1821. They made their way to a mission station run by another Scot, John Brownlee, at Chumie about seventy miles to the north-east of Grahamstown and between the Fish and Kei rivers. Brownlee himself had not been at Chumie for very long. He had been a missionary of the L.M.S. but had resigned from the society and been appointed as a government missionary agent. The situation was therefore a curious one. Brownlee and Thomson were both paid by the government. Yet Thomson and Bennie were both in some sense missionaries of the Glasgow Society. And for a while the three men worked together on the same station, itinerating amongst the neighbouring villages and gradually

7

collecting a small group of catechumens. From the very start a school formed part of their mission.

In 1823 the three were joined by John Ross, the first man to be formally ordained by the Church of Scotland for missions to the heathen abroad. He brought with him a small printing press. It was to be Bennie's great work to be one of the pioneers in reducing the Xhosa language to writing and in producing a literature in that language. Hand in hand with the development of a written language and the books containing it went the necessary education to make the people literate. But the main purpose of this education was always evangelization and the men at Chumie believed that so-called native agents and teachers would be indispensable for the work. By the end of 1823 several of these lay but indigenous ministers were already being employed. The number of outstations grew and it was soon possible to think in terms of setting up a new chief station which could become the centre of its own network. At the end of 1824 Bennie and Ross, as the representatives of the Glasgow Society, moved about a dozen miles to the south-east and there established a station which was to be called "Lovedale" after Thomas Love.

Lovedale passed through almost every imaginable vicissitude. The station was destroyed and its site moved, and it was not until 1841 that the present institution of Lovedale was really established. The Moravian example, as was the case in almost all South African mission stations, played some part in the planning of this new missionary centre.

By this time the Glasgow Society's work in southern Africa had grown. The Scots had encouraged the use of native agents and needed a seminary where these men could be trained. The L.M.S. also discussed the possibilities of setting up some such institution at about the same time. It was a sign that Christian missions had rooted themselves in the country and that a new generation of people were growing up for whom Christianity was not just something brought by men from Europe. On the whole the Churches and missionary organizations in the sub-continent were not quick to develop an indigenous ministry but the very heart of the Lovedale institution was its seminary. Nor must this seminary be thought of as a post-graduate divinity school.

Training African missionaries involved teaching them the basic things like reading and writing. A whole scheme of education from start to finish was necessary.

Hardly had the institution been conceived than Scottish missions were badly shaken by ecclesiastical disputes in Scotland. The great debate about the state connection led to one division after another within the Scottish Church. The work in South Africa was split in two. Part of the work became a missionary undertaking of the Free Church of Scotland. The other part was taken under the wing of the United Presbyterian Church. Lovedale itself was allotted the first of these and William Govan was sent out to South Africa in 1840 to be principal of the institution.

When at last the institution was opened, Govan insisted that the educational facilities it offered should be open to members of all denominations and all races. In the nineteenth century Cape colony there was nothing unusual in this mixing of black and white at school. At Lovedale separate dining tables and dormitories were provided but school classes were common. Since educational facilities in the colony as a whole were still undeveloped, white parents were glad to be able to send their children to missionary institutions. Lovedale produced some of the outstanding white leaders of colonial government and society of the next generation.

Govan's principalship was soon interrupted by one of the periodic frontier wars. Govan, indeed, returned to Scotland believing that it would be years before the work could be resumed. Early in 1850 he was back at Lovedale. It was not the last time that war was to threaten the institution. All missionary life and work along the frontier was subject to continual disturbance. But the institution continued to grow. Sir George Grey's plans for using missions to settle the frontier area benefited Lovedale and led to the expansion of the manual training side of the work. Moves towards unity in Scotland made it possible for increased financial support to be provided. By 1863 pupils were being trained as blacksmiths, carpenters, printers and bookbinders, teachers and missionaries. "A very superior English, classical, and mathematical education" was being provided.

Govan was succeeded as principal by James Stewart in 1870. Stewart, an Edinburgh Scot by birth, was drawn to missionary work by reading Livingstone's diaries. He accompanied Livingstone to the Zambesi in 1862. On his return to Scotland he was ordained and in 1867 was appointed to the staff of Lovedale. His relations with his predecessor, especially over the future development of the institution, led to dispute. Govan disagreed with Stewart's ideas because he believed that African ministers should possess precisely the same qualifications as Europeans and was disinclined to accept Stewart's belief in a "two-stream" system which would supply a large number of African Christians, moderately well-equipped for pastoral work, and a small class of highly educated African Christians to provide leaders for the next generation. Stewart's views, perhaps more realistic in the circumstances, eventually prevailed, and he remained principal of Lovedale until 1905.

Under his leadership the institution became perhaps the foremost educational centre in all southern Africa. The declared aim of Lovedale was to teach trades and crafts and to produce preachers and teachers. But there was also an emphasis upon strict and high academic standards and upon having properly qualified lay men and women on the staff. The institution continued to provide a common education for black and white pupils and there was a deliberate mixing of the races so that they might come to know one another. A hospital was eventually added to all the other activities of the institution and became the first place in the country at which Africans could be fully trained as nurses. In a sense all higher education for Africans emanated from Lovedale, including the first university college, though this was not opened until 1916, eleven years after Stewart's death.

Of course it is true that Lovedale was not the only institution of its kind in southern Africa. The Methodist Healdtown and the Anglican St Matthew's are neither of them very far from Lovedale and both were institutions of much the same type, until the Bantu Education Act of 1953 virtually put an end to the era of missionary education. And all over the country there were other establishments of a similar kind run by various denominations. For well over a hundred years African education was in the hands of the Churches (usually supported by government grants) and was at times far in advance of anything else in the country.

Lovedale has been singled out for special attention partly because its history has been published in a full and scholarly form, but more especially because the great contribution of Scottish missionaries ought to be recognized.

Educational missionary institutions introduced a new type of missionary strategy. Here were mission stations which were just as much complete societies in themselves as any of the older settlements, but because of the emphasis upon education they could never become entirely closed or "insulated". A continuous flow of people from outside passed through the institution, lived for some years in a Christian environment, and then went out to towns and villages outside, often to occupy positions of relative influence and importance. It was a new way, as it were, of spreading the gospel.

Inevitably this type of mission has been subjected to criticism. The system has been condemned as a sort of bribery, or an attempt to coat the pill of the gospel with a sugar of educational or medical service. The education provided has itself been described as the embodiment of paternalism or the imposition of a foreign culture upon a people whose own traditions were thereby destroyed. It has also been condemned, of course, as being too "liberal" and helping to create political agitation. None of these criticisms can alter the fact that such missionary institutions were of enormous importance in the history of Christianity and education in southern Africa.

14. Ethiopianism: Christianity and Politics

One of the most obvious features of the modern South African religious scene is the number and variety of the so-called separatist sects. The "sects" have been classified as belonging to three types. The two older types are the Ethiopian and the Zionist, distinguished from each other by the fact that, while the Ethiopian groups are "orthodox" in teaching, the Zionists have retained some elements of traditional African paganism along with a rather Pentecostalist kind of Christianity. Amongst the Zionists will usually be found an emphasis upon purificatory rites, speaking with tongues, ritual taboos, healing ceremonies, and often an admixture of the jazz culture of the cities. The third type is Messianism and this will be discussed in a later chapter. For the moment we shall be looking at the older types which were often in the early days simply described as Ethiopianism.

What was probably the first secession took place in Basutoland in 1872. There had been a good deal of political unrest in the territory over its relationship with the Cape Colony, but it is not clear whether this had any direct connection with the schism. About 150 members of the Paris Evangelical Missionary Society congregation at Mount Hermon broke away from the control of the society and declared that they would no longer be bound by any regulations other than those made by themselves. The schism did not last very long but it made a considerable impression on Europeans who regarded it as politically sinister. It is worth noting three factors in the situation which were to recur frequently in future secessions—the resentment of white control, the possible political implications, and the resistance to disciplinary regulations.

The first permanent secession was the Tembu National Church

founded by Nehemiah Tile. Tile was a Tembu who had been ordained as a Methodist minister after being trained at Heald-town. In 1884, with the support of the Tembu paramount chief and after a quarrel with the superintendent of the circuit, Tile set up his Church. The paramount chief was enthroned as the visible head of the Church on earth and there were a large number of converts from Methodism and other bodies. The chief seems to have regarded the whole affair as a way of enhancing his own importance and prestige and of creating a new national feeling amongst his people (one of the tribes in the Transkei which had by this time been annexed to the Cape Colony). Government pressure was brought to bear on him, however, and he renounced the movement which lost a good deal of its impetus as a result.

There were other similar movements elsewhere including one notable schism in Sekukuniland in the Transvaal. Here a white missionary of the Berlin Society called Winter (see Chapter 11) led the seceders. He maintained that missionaries treated even educated Africans as inferiors and that it was necessary to create independent Churches which could be governed by Africans. Nemesis, in the shape of the logic of his own arguments, soon overtook Winter. No sooner had the new Church been constituted than it denounced and dismissed its own founder as an intruder.

The first time the actual word Ethiopian was used in connec-tion with a seceding body was in the case of a schism in the Methodist Church in 1892. A minister called Mangena Mokoni set up his Ethiopian Church in the Transvaal because he believed that Africans were not being given equal rights with Europeans within the Methodist organization. It is important to notice the differences between Mokoni's movement and the earlier seces-sions. These had been "national" in the sense that they were *tribal*, confined to a particular people in a particular area. The Ethiopian Church was "national" in a racial sense. It was an African Church and aimed at being *the* religious organization for all Africans in the sub-continent. Mokoni's appeal was to a racial nationalism wider than any of the little states of contemporary southern Africa.

He gained adherents rapidly. True to his ideal of an African Church, he tried to make his movement comprehensive rather than fissiparous. He tried to make contact with Tile's Tembu Church and eventually approached the American all-Negro African Methodist Episcopal Church in the hope that some kind of union could be negotiated. By this time Mokoni had been joined by another Methodist minister, James Dwane, the son of a sub-chief from the Eastern Cape who, like Tile, had been educated at Healdtown. Dwane was a man of considerable brilliance and gifts of leadership, ambitious and determined. When the union with the American body was agreed to in 1896 Dwane, by dint of getting to America first, was made general superintendent and eventually vicar-bishop for South Africa. Mokoni had been eclipsed within his own movement.

Dwane, however, remained unsatisfied. He felt that the Americans wanted too much control. He made a study of episcopacy and began to doubt the validity of his own orders. After a long delay and much hesitation on both sides, he led a very large number of Ethiopians into the Anglican Church. The vast majority of Mokoni's supporters from the Eastern Cape were thus formed into the Order of Ethiopia which was to be part of the Anglican Church and yet to retain its own identity. The idea was to preserve the traditions of the Ethiopians and to make them into a missionary spearhead of the Church. It cannot be said that the experiment has been entirely successful. In the area from which most members of the Order came there are usually two Anglican churches close together, competing against each other, and a good deal of tension exists amongst African clergy between those who are "Church" and those who are "Order". No doubt there have been faults on both sides. The chief problems have been problems of authority and jurisdiction. Neither Dwane nor any of his successors have ever been bishops, though the Order clearly expected to be given its own episcopal head. There has also been continual friction about whether the Order ought to be extra-diocesan as well as extra-parochial. The union continues, but so do tensions, discussions, and negotiations.

In the twentieth century the separatist movement has grown rapidly. In 1904 it was reckoned that there were only three such independent bodies with a total of about 25,000 followers between them. By 1925 there appeared to be about 130 "sects", whereas the census of 1946 gave the number as about 1,300 with some 1,100,000 adherents. The number of "sects" is now calculated at well over 2,000, though the figures are always merely approximate because of the discrepancy between officially recognized bodies and those which simply exist without recognition or registration.

At the turn of the century, then, Ethiopianism was still small but rapidly growing. African opinion on the movement was divided. J. T. Jabavu (one of the leading figures of his generation, a prominent Christian layman and one of the first African journalists) described the separatists as succumbing to a madness as great and as destructive as that which had resulted in the great Cattle Killing of the 1850s. Others believed that secessions were necessary because Christianity was being used to browbeat Africans into a state of perpetual subjection and humiliation.

White opinion was no less disturbed. Ethiopianism seemed to be political because it stood for a rejection of white guidance and control. The colonial governments were deeply concerned. The outcome of the Anglo-Boer war had been the defeat of the republics and their transformation into British colonies. There were thus four colonies in southern Africa—the Cape, the Orange River Colony, the Transvaal, and Natal. All of them had been in some degree affected by the war and the Transvaal, in particular, was in great need of reconstruction and relief. The British government was faced with the task of reconciling the ex-republics and of rebuilding their economy and administration, and there was already talk of uniting all four colonies in a single self-governing state under the British crown. The "native problem" was necessarily one of the great issues of the time and Ethiopianism was regarded as part of it. It was under these circumstances that the colonies appointed a joint Native Affairs Commission early in this century.

The report of the commission dealt with Ethiopianism and the commission's opinion was that the movement was not a result of political agitation but a natural expression of a desire for ecclesiastical independence. This desire the commission refused to condemn, but it said that "in the case of a subject race such an aspiration, misdirected on the one hand by the leadership of ignorant and misguided men, and repressed by misunderstanding and harshness on the other, might be fraught with the seeds of racial mistrust and discontent".[1] The advice of the commission was that every effort should be made to raise the standards of education amongst the ministers of the "sects" and to try to encourage the "sects" to unite with each other.

John X. Merriman, son of an Anglican bishop and prime minister of the Cape, was particularly anxious that there should be no repression. The other colonies were less sympathetic. The Natal government suspected that preachers of the separatist bodies had been partly responsible for stirring up a rebellion which took place in 1906,[2] and restrictions were placed upon African clergy who were "not under European control". The other two colonies were equally suspicious of the separatists.

This was the situation when the Union of South Africa came into existence. A National Convention representing the four colonies drew up a draft bill to create the new state. This bill was approved by the colonial legislatures and enacted by the British parliament. Amongst the many extremely knotty problems which had to be considered were the "native problem", the "colour bar", and the franchise. The Cape had a more liberal franchise policy and fought hard to maintain it. None of the other colonies wanted non-whites to possess the vote at all. The Cape was grudgingly allowed to go its own way for the time being. Merriman protested bitterly against a constitution which entrenched the colour bar and also contained what was virtually a prayer for divine protection. Anglican, Baptist, Presbyterian, Methodist, and other Church leaders signed a letter which condemned, in no uncertain terms, the theory that political rights ought to be based on race or colour. It was the beginnings of a new relationship between the Churches and South African society at large.

What had really happened was that the so-called native problem had become an internal matter. Between 1850 and 1900 the independent African territory had been absorbed by the colonies

[1] See J. du Plessis, *A History of Christian Missions in South Africa*, Appendix II.
[2] See S. Marks, "Christian African Participation in the 1906 Zulu Rebellion", *Bulletin of the Society for African Church History*, Vol. II, No. 1, pp. 55f.

and the republics or had come directly under the protection of the British crown. The "native question" was no longer primarily a matter of keeping the tribes on one's frontier in a peaceful condition. Africans were now subjects if not citizens of the white South African states. The creation of a single Union of South Africa made the internal nature of the issue more obvious. The Churches began to express strong views about the rights of the indigenous peoples.

In the nineteenth century most Churches and missionary bodies had been more or less paternalistic in their outlook. They believed that Africans were not yet sufficiently mature to be given real responsibility in Church or State. After the Anglo-Boer war there were some Church leaders who protested against the British decision to return the non-white people of the Transvaal to Boer rule. But British liberals were so convinced that generosity to their former enemies was the wisest course that these protests were set aside.

By 1910, however, when the Union came into being, paternalism was very slowly beginning to pass out of fashion. It persisted for a long time in some quarters, but it was no longer taken for granted in missionary circles. The Christian Churches had built up a magnificent educational system. Unless Africans who had been trained in it were given responsibility and the opportunity to make use of their qualifications there was bound to be frustration. Moreover, after the First World War, Christian socialism and the sort of ideals for which men like William Temple stood began to affect the South African Churches. Housing, wages, food, clothing, medical facilities, education, public morals, social justice, and political rights were believed to be matters on which Christian opinion ought to be expressed. Church assemblies and synods began to pass resolutions on these matters. Christianity began to be proclaimed as a social gospel. The Churches tried, little by little, to act as a conscience for the nation.

So far as the separatist "sects" were concerned, however, the Churches had little to say. After Union the government continued to try to follow a policy which combined restriction with rewards for good behaviour. The Native Land Act of 1913 made it very difficult indeed for separatist bodies in Natal and the Transvaal to own any land. On the other hand the government offered to "recognize" those "sects" who fulfilled certain conditions, and recognition brought real material benefits to ministers of these bodies—cheaper tickets on the railways and licences as marriage officers.

But the situation was exacerbated by the growing prominence, after 1910, of the Zionist bodies. In 1920 a "sect" called the Israelites assembled at Bulhoek near Queenstown to keep the passover. They refused to return home but waited on for the coming of the millennium. They built themselves about 300 huts on crown land and would not be moved. Finally a force of 800 policemen was sent to disperse them. The Israelites were assured by their leaders that bullets could not hurt them. In the ensuing fight a large number of them were killed. All the old fears that the "sects" were politically dangerous revived. A commission was appointed to inquire into the whole matter. The commission exempted missionaries from blame but recognized that anti-white feeling was growing. There seemed no way of preventing this except by giving Africans their own Churches, alongside the "white" parent body, in which they would have complete responsibility.

This was, in fact, the policy adopted by the Dutch Reformed Church, but most other Churches continued to try and hold their black and white members together. In 1923, however, the Scottish missions tried an experiment along the lines suggested by the commission. At this time the South African missions were under the control of the United Free Church of Scotland. The stations stretched in a great semi-circle from the Eastern Cape through the Transkei and Natal into the Transvaal. These missions were now constituted as the Bantu Presbyterian Church. The arrangement has often been criticized as seeming to smell too much of *apartheid*, but at the time, against the background of the tensions over Ethiopianism and Zionism, it seemed the only way to encourage independence and responsibility amongst the African ministers. The mother Church in Scotland retained control over the institutions, which still needed a good deal of financial support. White missionaries continued to be sent out to South Africa to serve as ministers of the Bantu Presbyterian Church and their salaries were paid from Scotland. The Bantu Presbyterian Church took over direct control of the former mission stations and the stipends of African clergy became the responsibility of local Christians.

Government policy towards the "sects" continued along much the same lines as before. It was reluctant to grant recognition to new bodies and it tried to persuade the existing ones to amalgamate. Privileges like the right to buy wine for sacramental use, to be registered as marriage officers, railway concessions, and the ownership of land were jealously guarded. The government required a body to have been in existence for at least ten years, to possess a regular constitution, to show general signs of progress, to possess at least six congregations and a ministry with certain definite, though minimal, educational qualifications, moral integrity, and an ability to discharge civil functions. If these requirements were met, then it was possible for the body concerned to be recognized. Needless to say there were literally hundreds of "sects" which were quite unable to meet them and, in fact, made no attempt to do so. Those who are recognized are usually of the staider and more "orthodox" Ethiopian type. But Zionism is perhaps more vigorous and proliferates more exuberantly. There is nothing which makes the existence of such "sects" illegal. The fact that they are not recognized does not mean that they are proscribed; it merely means that they are denied the privileges extended to others. Attempts to make recognition more difficult to obtain does not prevent the growth of new sects—it may, indeed, encourage the existence of even greater numbers of unrecognized bodies. And it is in the unrecognized bodies that the greatest degree of indigenization, as popularly understood, is to be found. The worship and activities of the recognized sects are more often than not faithful copies of the imported Christianity of the missionaries.

15 Some Recent Developments

One of the most obvious features of South African Church history in this present century has been the great growth of Roman Catholic missions. The history of Roman Catholicism in the sub-continent really began in 1837 when Raymond Griffith was consecrated to be the first vicar apostolic for South Africa. He was instructed to devote his attention primarily to the care of those who were already Roman Catholics and neither he nor his successor gave much attention to the indigenous peoples. There were a few baptisms and in the 1840s a small mission station was established at Malmesbury in the Western Cape. Even these sporadic efforts caused Protestant grumblings about popish aggression. Both Dutch Reformed and Anglican authorities seem to have believed that white Roman Catholics should be allowed their own chaplains but that missionary activity ought not to be encouraged. On the other hand the Roman Catholics themselves gradually came to feel that Protestant missions were too much concerned with Bible-reading and psalm-singing and were not creating a Christian community involved in living the Christian life. Whether this judgment was justified or not, it led to a new determination to undertake extensive and organized missions to the heathen.

In the middle of the nineteenth century Bishop Ricards in the Eastern Cape played an important part in the systematic building up of a missionary policy. He planned to use members of religious communities who would establish mission settlements on the pattern of the work done by the Trappists in Algeria. Hitherto the general feeling amongst Roman Catholics had been that converts ought to be immediately and automatically integrated into the social structure of the "white" Church and colony. In the general state of affairs at the time this expectation was far too optimistic. Ricard's plan was to persuade African tribes to accept English law and Western civilization along with Christianity and so make it possible for integration to be effected in due course. The bishop's plans and ideals were probably better than the actual execution of them for, at any rate for some time, the scheme did not show any real fruits. At the same time another bishop, Allard, was instituting missions in Natal, round Pieter-maritzburg, and in Basutoland.

The most famous Roman Catholic mission centre was to be Marianhill, the Trappist settlement in Natal. Modelled on the monastic missions of early medieval Europe it became a show-place for what could be done in the settlement type of mission station. In concrete, descriptive terms it did not differ very much, perhaps, from the village settlements of other denominations except that it was more elaborate and that it had the religious community at its core. It set itself to cater for the whole man (not merely for his religious needs) and to raise the general standards of living amongst the converts attracted to it.

After 1922, when an apostolic delegate was first appointed, a greater cohesion and a new over-all planning was introduced into the work of the Roman Catholic Church in South Africa. A hier-archy, with four archbishops and a large number of other bishops, was established in 1951. There has been a marked increase in the number of adherents in recent years, amongst white South Africans as well as amongst the African population. Chains of mission stations have spread across central South Africa, in par-ticular, and Basutoland has become one of the most obviously "Catholic" parts of the sub-continent. An indigenous ministry, white and black, has grown rapidly. There are thriving seminaries and novitiates, containing large numbers of South Africans of all races, at a time when some other Churches are not finding it easy to attract local candidates to the ministry. The ordination of African clergy and bishops has been encouraged with an en-thusiasm which puts the rest of South African Christendom to shame.

It is said of South Africa, as of the rest of the continent, that it is Rome and the Pentecostalists who are making the greatest strides in missionary expansion. But there is little published information available about the Pentecostalist bodies. It is probable that most of them do not do a great deal of what is usually regarded as "mission" work—i.e. work amongst non-Christian Africans—but perhaps the rapid spread of Zionism is, in a sense, the equivalent of the growth and development of Pentecostalist groups amongst whites.

This century has also seen the development of important new trends in the missionary policy of the Dutch Reformed Church. After the Anglo-Boer war and despite the disappearance of the old northern republics, an Afrikaner national consciousness persisted as a powerful political, religious and cultural force. There was a movement towards closer unity amongst the Dutch Reformed Churches of the four colonies and in 1905 a conference was held at which a federal constitution was framed. (This did not, of course, affect either the *Hervormde Kerke* or the *Gereformeerde Kerk*, but only the Dutch Reformed Churches proper). In 1911 an enabling act of the new Union Parliament made provision for a complete organic union of the Dutch Reformed Churches, which the various synods had already approved in principle. But the consent of the consistories was required and in the Orange Free State and the Transvaal the proposal was defeated, perhaps because political suspicion of the Cape Church was not yet dead. Mission work was, therefore, hampered by the fact that it had to be planned and executed by means of complicated federal machinery.

(The project for a single organic union of the Dutch Reformed Churches was never entirely abandoned. It was recently taken up again with more success and in the past few years there has at last been a single synod with a single moderator for the Church throughout South Africa.)

Meanwhile the rise of Ethiopianism in the early twentieth century seems to have made a great impression on the missionary planners of the Dutch Reformed Church. There was a real fear that the ordination of African ministers might lead to secessions. And there was also a great deal of suspicion that political unrest lay behind Ethiopian demands for independence. Nevertheless the Dutch Reformed Churches had begun to adopt the principle of separate development. It seemed to them, as to the Scottish missionaries, that this was the proper way to encourage African aspirations and an indigenous Church and ministry. Separate synods for the "mother" Church (i.e. whites) and the "mission" Church had been held as early as 1880, though in the Cape it was at first a matter of convenience rather than principle that the mission Church should be separately organized.

About 1905 there was a great burst of missionary activity which led to the creation of missions in Ceylon, Rhodesia, and East Africa, as well as at home. By the time of Union there were fifty-two missionaries in South Africa and thirty-seven abroad, and the number of converts was reckoned at about 125,000. New missionary activity produced new thinking about missions and, in 1932, the Cape synod produced an official statement which argued that the conversion of the heathen must be followed by the institution of a Church for the converts. Congregations must become self-supporting. Aspirations towards full independence would inevitably follow and the "mother" Church must not try to frustrate them. Nor must it de-nationalize the converts or destroy their indigenous culture. Therefore an independent and separate Church was the obvious answer. Since then all Dutch Reformed work in South Africa has been based upon this policy of separation.

The problems caused by conflicting denominational missions played their part, all over the world, in the rise of the ecumenical movement. The scandal of division, accepted because so familiar in Europe, seemed much more obvious in the so-called mission fields. This was true in South Africa also. In earlier chapters there has been some account of the kind of conflict that developed. By the early years of this century missionaries had begun to feel that something must be done to reduce friction and tension. In 1904, largely through the leadership of James Stewart of Lovedale, the South African General Missionary Conference was founded. This was the period when the first steps were being taken towards the international and interdenominational missionary gathering at Edinburgh in 1910, which was such a landmark in the history of ecumenism and missions. The South African body was, in a sense, an anticipation of the Christian Councils which were to

8

come into existence as a result of the Edinburgh meetings. It consisted of members from missionary societies as well as Churches and it included Anglican and Dutch Reformed representatives. Both these bodies had, for different reasons, refused to support earlier attempts at interdenominational organization and both remained somewhat hesitant even about this new venture. Roman Catholics did not belong to it and nor did representatives of the African "separatist sects". These last were not really regarded as being part of Christendom and were far more talked about than talked with by the Conference. At its first session it described the sects as "striking at the foundation of all missionary work".

The Conference met eight times between 1904 and 1932. It laid down a doctrinal basis of co-operation and membership, a basis which reflected the very conservative theology of most of the members. Great stress was laid upon the Bible as the inspired word of God, upon the power of angels and devils, and upon the resurrection of the body, as well as upon the usual basic doctrines such as the Trinity and the Incarnation. The Conference discussed such things as how to reach areas which were not being evangelized, whether there ought to be a gentleman's agreement to divide the country amongst various denominations, mutual recognition, the relationship between missions and education, polygamy, and the "sects". The minutes suggest that the Conference helped to create better relations between Christians on a personal level, but they also indicate that some members did not take the Conference very seriously and its practical achievements were not spectacular.

By 1932, as a result of Edinburgh and subsequent conferences, the International Missionary Council had come into existence, consisting of missionary societies as well as of Churches, and rather conservative in outlook. Christian Councils had been established under its aegis in many parts of the world. At the same time the ecumenical movement had produced two other associations, "Life and Work" and "Faith and Order", which were not so immediately concerned with "missions" and whose membership was confined to representatives of Churches. Steps were already being taken to amalgamate these two movements in the World Council of Churches, though this was actually to be delayed by the outbreak of the Second World War.

In 1934 J. R. Mott, who had probably been chiefly responsible for Edinburgh 1910 and was one of the leading figures in the ecumenical movement, visited South Africa. The question of re-organizing the South African General Conference had already been raised at its meeting in 1932. A "National Christian Council" had been suggested, which would include "native Christians" as well as "missionaries". Mott now proposed that there should be a local Christian Council affiliated to the I.M.C. and this body was actually launched at Bloemfontein in 1936 as "an association of Churches and Missionary Societies of South Africa for the Extension of the Kingdom of God". There was some initial Dutch Reformed participation in the new body, but in 1941 issues of language and colour led to their withdrawal and the Council really became representative of English-speaking non-Roman Christianity.

The amalgamation of the I.M.C. with the World Council of Churches has led, in the 1960s, to further reorganization. Attempts have been made to increase co-operation with the Afrikaans Churches and the Roman Catholics and also with some of the "separatist sects" who have recently formed themselves into a body called the African Independent Churches Association. There are other, perhaps more exciting, ecumenical developments taking place at the same time. Anglicans, Congregationalists, Methodists, and Presbyterians have co-operated in establishing a Federal Theological Seminary for the training of African clergy, as well as in helping to endow a faculty of theology at one of the universities. Conversations are currently proceeding between representatives of various denominations. These conversations are somewhat out of date in their approach but there are signs that they may soon begin to escape from the strait-jacket of denominational bargaining which has hitherto seemed to be characteristic of them. The Theological Education Fund of the I.M.C. has been sponsoring a series of summer schools for the staff of theological colleges and seminaries, in which Roman Catholic participation is a notable feature. And members of all the Churches have supported the Christian Institute, a recent association set up to encourage ecumenism and Christian concern in social problems.

The "separatist sects" show no signs of losing their ability to proliferate. Healing movements of considerable size have developed, some of them within the "orthodox" Churches. In these movements the prominence of women healers is a significant feature and this may be linked with the great importance of African women's organizations generally, within the "Churches" as well as the "sects". These women's organizations have always been extremely powerful, constituting a sort of *élite* within the Christian community. They now seem to be showing signs of becoming *ecclesiolae*, holding all-night prayer meetings within locked churches from which even the clergy are excluded.

But probably the most significant recent development in this sphere is the rise of the so-called Messianic movements. These new "sects" are what their name suggests. They offer a new Messiah—a black Messiah—as an alternative to the "white" Christ. It is argued that the white Christian does not appear to love the black man. Can the white Christian's God, then, love the black man? Ought not the black man to have his own God, his own Christ?

Isaiah Shembe's Nazareth Movement is a case in point. Isaiah Shembe died a few years ago and his son now leads the movement. Shembe himself has become a quasi-divine figure. He is spoken of in language which suggests that he is a kind of Melchizedek-cum-Christ type. His birth was not normal and human. His origins are unknown. He was born of the Spirit. He was Spirit. He was not of the world but of heaven. He was a servant sent by God and through him we know that God is not beyond the ocean but here, among us.

The obvious political and social factors which have given rise to such movements bring us to a last and most imporant matter which it is not yet possible for an historian to deal with adequately. The *apartheid* policy of the South African government is so well known that, perhaps, it is not necessary to do more than merely touch upon some of its aspects as it affects the Churches.

The National Party swept to victory in a landslide election in 1948. The new government propounded the theory of *apartheid* ("separate development" of the races) as its solution to the social problems of the country. Segregation was not new, of course. Social segregation had existed in fact for several centuries. Economically there were sharp differences between the races. In the nineteenth and early twentieth centuries the Cape had had a strong liberal tradition, but otherwise there had been no equality in political rights. *Apartheid* must not, therefore, be regarded as the sole cause of disunity and tensions between black and white. It was advanced as the government's answer to the problems. The only way to maintain peace and preserve "white civilization" is to separate the races in every way, socially, politically, economically, geographically.

The Christian Churches are necessarily involved in the social problems. We have seen how in this present century Christian leaders in South Africa had come to see the social implications of the gospel. A concern with poverty, housing, conditions of employment, justice, and human rights had become characteristic of official Christian assemblies. Moreover the Churches had developed a network of educational institutions for the non-white peoples all over the country. By educating men and women and helping them to realize their potentials, Christians were, in a sense, responsible for creating frustrations and tensions. African graduates might find themselves without the opportunity to use their abilities and qualifications. The existence of the "sects" was proof that this frustration was present even within the Churches. It was virtually impossible for Africans and other non-white people to reach positions of leadership in any sphere. As paternalism declined within the Churches such a situation became more and more uncomfortable.

For all these reasons there was already a good deal of unhappiness in Christian circles before 1948. After the inception of the programme of *apartheid*, this unease became much sharper. Absolute segregation was proposed as the only possible solution to the country's problems. Inevitably such a policy requires a high degree of state control over the lives of individuals. People's homes, jobs, education, transport, political organizations, and churches have to be controlled and kept separate on a racial basis. Moreover the government regards the situation as so critical, and

the need for *apartheid* as a solution so urgent, that it has frequently said that South Africa is in a position analogous to that
of a state of war. Opposition and criticism should therefore be
regarded as potentially subversive and criminal and the normal
rule of law is suspended as in wartime.

To many Christians the rigid separation of the races seems to
be a denial of the Christian ideal of love. So absolute a degree of
state control seems derogatory to the dignity of the human indi-
vidual. Discrimination seems to humiliate some of God's crea-
tures. Justice seems often to be totally disregarded. Over and over
again synods and assemblies of the Churches have made pro-
nouncements to this effect.

Yet it must be said that there are many Christians in South
Africa (perhaps the majority of white Christians) who do not feel
this. Statements made by the Dutch Reformed Church show that,
on the whole, it has no great moral difficulty over *apartheid*. Its
own missionary theory is not dissimilar, and it inclines to the view
that there ought to be no mixing of the races but that equality
and justice ought to be secured for members of each race separately.
A large number of white laymen in other denominations probably
feel that politics is a field into which the Church ought not to
trespass, that the traditional, *de facto*, social segregation ought to
be preserved and that a dangerous explosion might follow from
any attempt to reverse the present policies. Perhaps the greatest
problem in the Churches is the preservation of a real spirit of
unity in the face of growing distrust, fear, and even hatred between
Christians of different races.

There are other problems, too. The Group Areas Act of 1950,
the cornerstone of *apartheid*, provides for strict social and geographical segregation. Whole sections of the population may be
moved from one part of a town to another. Churches become re-
dundant in one area and are desperately needed in another. A
clergyman may not be able to live in his parish if the people are
of another race. It becomes increasingly difficult for the different
races to worship together, even where this has been the tradition.
The Native Laws Amendment Act of 1957 contained a clause
allowing the government to declare a church building out of
bounds to members of particular racial groups. It seems likely

that if Africans were to become trustees for Church property the Church might not be allowed to own land or buildings in "white" areas. Since the Bantu Education Act of 1953 the Churches have found it virtually impossible to maintain their educational institutions. Mission work has had to be almost completely reorganized. And since great stress is now laid upon the importance of "mother-tongue" education, Christians may soon find themselves deeply divided by a sort of latter-day curse of Babel. These are practical problems; the fundamental issue is the meaning of Christian love. What the final outcome will be is not a matter for the historian to guess at.

Select Bibliography

GENERAL

W. E. Brown, *The Catholic Church in South Africa* (Burns & Oates, 1960).

J. du Plessis, *History of Christian Missions in South Africa* (Longmans, 1911).

H. Davies, *Great South African Christians* (O.U.P., 1951).

S. P. Engelbrecht, *Geskiedenis van die Nederduits Hervormde Kerk van Afrika* (J. H. de Bussy, 2nd Ed., 1936).

G. P. Ferguson, *The Story of the Congregational Union of South Africa* (Pretoria, 1940).

G. B. A. Gerdener, *Recent Developments in the South African Mission Field* (N. G. Kerk-Uitgewers, 1958).

L. A. Hewson, *An Introduction to South African Methodists* (Cape Town, 1951).

P. Hinchliff, *The Anglican Church in South Africa* (Darton, Longman & Todd, 1963).

J. P. Jooste, *Die Geskiedenis van die Gereformeerde Kerk in Suid Afrika, 1859–1959* (Potchefstroom, 1959).

C. Lewis & G. E. Edwards, *The Historical Records of the Church of the Province of South Africa* (S.P.C.K., 1934).

A. Moorrees, *Die Nederduitse Gereformeerde Kerk in Suid Afrika, 1652–1873* (S. A. Bybelvereniging, 1937).

W. J. van der Merwe, *Development of Missionary Attitudes in the Dutch Reformed Church in South Africa* (Nasionale Pers, 1936).

E. A. Walker, *History of Southern Africa* (Longmans, 3rd Ed., 1957).

J. Whiteside, *The History of the Wesleyan Methodist Church of South Africa* (Juta, 1906).

CHAPTER 1

T. N. Hanekom, *Helperus Ritzema van Lier* (N. G. Kerk-Uitgewers, 1959).

CHAPTER 2

B. Kruger, *The Pear Tree Blossoms* (Moravian Mission Press, 1968).

CHAPTER 3

A. Dreyer, *Boustowwe vir die Geskiedenis van die Nederduitse Gereformeerde Kerk in Suid Afrika* (N.G.K. 1936, Vol. III).
J. A. Hewitt, *Sketches of English Church History in South Africa* (Juta, 1887).
A. D. Pont, "Oor die Kerkwet van 1862", *Hervormde Teologiese Studies* (October 1963, pp. 36f).

CHAPTER 4

D. R. Briggs, *An Historical Survey of the Bethelsdorp Mission of the L.M.S.*, unpublished thesis, Rhodes University, Grahamstown, B.D.
P. Hinchliff, *A Calendar of Cape Missionary Correspondence, 1800–1850* (National Council for Social Research, 1967).
S. P. Engelbrecht, "Niks Nuuts onder die Son", *Hervormde Teologiese Studies*, XVI.
R. Lovett, *History of the London Missionary Society, 1795–1885* (2 vols. O.U.P., 1899).
W. M. Macmillan, *The Cape Colour Question* (Faber & Gwyer, 1927).
W. M. Macmillan, *Bantu, Boer, and Briton* (Faber & Gwyer, 1929: new edition, Clarendon, 1963).

CHAPTER 5

W. B. Boyce, *Memoir of the Rev. William Shaw* (Wesleyan Conference Office, 1874).
W. Shaw, *The Story of My Mission in South-Eastern Africa* (Hamilton, Adams and Co., 1860).

CHAPTER 6

J. A. I. Agar Hamilton, *The Native Policy of the Voortrekkers* (Maskew Miller, 1928).
A. Dreyer, *Die Kaapse Kerk en die Groot Trek* (Cape Town, 1929).
S. P. Engelbrecht, *Die Kaapse Predikante van die Sewentiende en Agtiende Eeue* (de Bussy, 1952).
G. B. A. Gerdener, *Boustowwe vir die Geskiedenis van die Nederduits-Gereformeerde Kerk in die Transgariep* (Nasionale Pers, 1930).

E. W. Smith, *Life and Times of Daniel Lindley* (Epworth Press, 1949).

B. Spoelstra, *Die Doppers in Suid Afrika* (Nasionale Boekhandel, 1963).

E. A. Walker, *The Great Trek* (A. & C. Black, 1934).

CHAPTER 7

G. Callaway, *A Shepherd of the Veld* (Wells Gardner, Darton and Co., 1912).

D. G. L. Cragg, *The Relations of the Amapondo and the Colonial Authorities (1830–1886), with special reference to the role of the Wesleyan Missionaries* (unpublished thesis, University of Oxford, D.Phil.).

A. E. du Toit, *The Cape Frontier* (Government Printer, Cape Town, 1954).

P. Hinchliff, *Calendar of Cape Missionary Correspondence, 1800–1850* (National Council for Social Research, 1967).

N. Majeke, *The Role of the Missionaries in Conquest* (Society of Young Africa, undated).

T. Matshikiza, "The Role of the Missionary in the Conquest of South Africa", *Prism*, No. 63.

J. Rutherford, *Sir George Grey* (Cassell, 1961).

B. E. Seton, *Wesleyan Missions and the Sixth Frontier War* (unpublished thesis, Cape Town University, Ph.D.).

C. Uys, *In the Era of Shepstone* (Lovedale Press, 1933).

CHAPTER 8

R. Coupland, *Livingstone's Last Journey* (Collins, 1945).

W. O. Chadwick, *Mackenzie's Grave* (Hodder & Stoughton, 1959).

S. P. Engelbrecht, "Niks Nuuts onder die Son", *Hervormde Teologiese Studies* XVI.

D. Livingstone, *Missionary Travels and Researches in South Africa* (Harper, 1858).

J. I. Macnair, *Livingstone's Travels* (Dent, 1954).

H. L. Pretorius, "Livingstone en die Boers", *Ned. Geref. Teologiese Tydskrif*, VIII, pp. 29f.

J. A. Sharp, *David Livingstone, Missionary and Explorer* (Epworth, 1920).

CHAPTER 9

S. J. Botha, "Die Historiese Agtergrond van die Kerkwet van 1862", *Hervormde Teologiese Studies*, XIX, pp. 25f.

A. Dreyer, *Die Kaapse Kerk en die Groot Trek* (Cape Town 1929).

G. B. A. Gerdener, *Boustowwe vir die Geskiedenis van die Nederduits-Gereformeerde Kerk in die Transgariep* (Nasionale Pers, 1930).

B. R. Kruger, "Die Aandeel van die Ou Gereformeerdes in die Inlywing onder die Kaapse Sinode", *Hervormde Teologiese Studies*, XVI, pp. 66f.

A. D. Pont, "Oor die Kerkwet van 1862", *Hervormde Teologiese Studies*, XIX, pp. 36f.

And certain documents reprinted in *Hervormde Teologiese Studies*, XVI, pp. 105f. and XVIII, pp. 153f.

CHAPTER 10

B. B. Burnett, *The Missionary Work of the First Anglican Bishop of Natal* (unpublished thesis, Rhodes University, Grahamstown).

G. W. Cox, *Life of Bishop Colenso* (Ridgeway, 2 Vols. 1888).

P. Hinchliff, *John William Colenso, Bishop of Natal* (Nelson, 1964).

M. A. Hooker, *The Place of Bishop Colenso in South African History* (unpublished thesis, University of the Witwatersrand).

W. Rees, *Colenso Letters from Natal* (Shuter & Shooter, 1958).

CHAPTER 11

D. P. Dugmore, *The Beginnings of Methodist Missionary Policy in the Transvaal* (unpublished thesis, Pretoria University, M.A.).

I am also much indebted to D. C. Veysie for allowing me to see material collected by him for a Ph.D. thesis at Rhodes University on Methodism in the Transvaal in the nineteenth century.

CHAPTER 12

W. M. Douglas, *Andrew Murray and his Message* (Oliphant, no date).

J. du Plessis, *Life of Andrew Murray* (Marshall, 1919).

CHAPTER 13

R. H. W. Shepherd, *Lovedale, South Africa, 1841–1941* (Lovedale Press, undated).

H. Davies & R. H. W. Shepherd, *South African Missions, 1800–1950* (Thomas Nelson, 1954).

J. Wells, *Stewart of Lovedale* (Hodder & Stoughton, 1909).

CHAPTER 14

E. Roux, *Time Longer than Rope* (University of Wisconsin, 1964).

B. Sundkler, *Bantu Prophets in South Africa* (Lutterworth, 1948).

T. Verryn, *A History of the Order of Ethiopia* (unpublished thesis, Church of the Province of South Africa, A.Th.).

CHAPTER 15

Statements on Race Relations, Dutch Reformed Church Information Bureau, 1960.

L. Cawood, *The Churches and Race Relations in South Africa* (Institute of Race Relations, 1964).

A. A. Dubb, *The Role of the Church in an Urban African Society* (unpublished thesis, Rhodes University, M.A.; to be published).

T. G. V. Inman, unpublished Kellogg Lectures, delivered at the Episcopal Theological School, 1963: "The Ecumenical Task in South Africa."

M. L. Martin, *The Biblical Concept of Messiahs and Messianism in Southern Africa* (Morija Press, 1964).

B. A. Paauw, *Bantu Christians and their Churches* (O.U.P.: in preparation).

B. Sundkler, *The Christian Ministry in Africa* (S.C.M., 1960).

Index

Aboriginees Protection Society, 71
Africans, 2, 13, 23, 30f, 34, 37, 39,
    43ff, 47ff, 50, 54ff, 66, 69f, 73, 76ff,
    85, 87f, 90f, 93ff, 97, 99, 102, 107
    (*see also* Bantu, Nguni, Pondos,
    Xhosas, etc.)
African Methodist Episcopal Church,
    92
Afrikaner, 84, 100
Agape, 10
Allard, Bp, 99
American Board of Missions, 42, 73,
    92
Amsterdam, 10, 14f, 17
Anglicans, 14ff, 18, 20ff, 29, 32f, 47,
    56f, 69, 71ff, 76ff, 83, 88, 92, 94, 98,
    102f
Anglo-Boer war, 78, 93, 95, 100
Apartheid, 27, 46, 96, 104ff
Apprenticeship, 26
Arab, 54
Archbell, Rev. J., 41
Armstrong, Bp, 48f
Assemblies, ecclesiastical, 17, 95, 106
Assistant missionaries, 77
Australia, 44

Bantu, 1
Bantu Education Act, 88, 107
Bantu Presbyterian Church, 96
Bapedi, 76
Baptism, 4, 9f, 15, 66f
Baptists, 94

Canterbury, Abp of, 67f
Cape of Good Hope, 2f, 5f, 8, 10, 13ff,
    16ff, 24, 27, 29, 33, 36, 43, 47, 49,
    61ff, 72, 74ff, 79f, 85, 90, 92ff, 98,
    105
Cape Church (*see* Dutch Reformed
    Church)
Cape Town, 8, 10, 13, 17, 43, 53, 55f,

Carnarvon, Lord, 75f
Casalis, E, 73
"Cattle Killing", 48, 93
Cetshwayo, 70f
Ceylon, 101
Chesson, F. W., 71
Christian Council, 101ff
Christian Institute, 103
Christian Reformed Church, 63f
Chumie, 85f
Cilliers, S., 41, 58f
Clarkebury, 33
Clergy, the, 15, 17ff, 32, 39f, 42, 48,
    60f, 63, 69, 75, 78ff, 84, 92, 94, 97,
    103 (*see also* Predikants)
Colenso, Bp, 65, 67ff, 70f, 73f,
    81
Colonial Bishoprics Fund, 69
Colonial chaplains, 8, 20
Colonial Office, 20
Colonists (*see* Settlers)
Coloured people, 53, 72
Commerce, 1, 14, 54f
Common Prayer, Book of, 32
Congregationalists, 103
Consistory, 17
Council of Seventeen, 3
Culture, 12

de Mist, Commissioner-General, 16f,
    19, 24
Diamonds, 75
Dingane, 39
Dissenters, 29
Doppers, 39f, 59, 62ff
Dort, Synod of, 4, 63f
Drakensberg, 39, 42, 60
Drakenstein, 6, 8
D'Urban, Sir B., 37f
Durban, 66
Dutch, 1f, 4, 6f, 15f, 18, 30
Dutch East India Company, 2f, 6, 9f,
    13f, 16

1

Dutch Reformed Church, 4ff, 8f, 13f, 16ff, 30, 34, 39f, 42, 58ff, 61f, 75, 79ff, 96, 98, 100ff, 106
Dwane, Rev. J., 92

East Africa, 101
Ecumenical movement, 102
"Edinburgh 1910", 101ff
Education, 35, 45, 59, 85ff, 95, 97, 105
Edwards, Rev. E., 73
England, Church of, 19, 29, 32 (*see also* Anglicans)
Enthusiasm, 22, 29
Erastianism, 63, 80f, 83
Established Church, 14, 19f, 22, 34, 62 (*see also* State Church)
Ethiopianism, 90ff, 96f, 100
Ethiopia, Order of, 92
Eva, 5
Evangelicals, 22, 26f, 79f, 84
Exeter Hall, 53

Farmers, 25f, 36ff
Faure, Ds A., 42
Federation, 44f, 75
Fish River, 13, 31, 37, 85
France, 13
Free Church of Scotland, 79, 87
Free Protestant Church, 83
Free trade, 43
French, 16, 18
Frontiers, 18, 23, 25, 32, 36ff, 45, 49, 60, 82, 87, 95

Gaika, 23
Genadendal, 10f
Gereformeerde Kerk, 64, 75, 100
Glasgow Missionary Society, 85f
Glenelg, Lord, 27, 38
Govan, Rev. W., 87f
Government agents, 49
Graaff Reinet, 15, 17, 23
Grahamstown, 32, 48f, 85
Gray, Bp, 47, 56, 65ff, 74, 83
Green, Dean, 67
Grey, Sir G., 43f, 46ff, 87
Griffith, Bp, 98
Griquas, 38, 43, 73, 75
Group Areas Act, 106

Healdtown, 88, 91f
Herrnhut, 9, 12
Hervormde Kerk, 62, 64, 100

High Commissioner, 44
Holland, 2, 4, 13, 17, 19, 32, 79, 82
Hottentots, 1f, 4f, 8ff, 16, 23ff, 27, 36, 38, 40, 73
Huguenots, 6
Hymns, 39f, 62ff

Indigenization, 97, 101
International Missionary Council, 102f

Jabavu, J. T., 93
Janssens, Governor, 16, 18, 24
Jenkins, Rev. T., 49

Kalahari, 53
Kei River, 33, 37, 49f, 85
Keiskamma River, 31, 43
Kolobeng, 53, 55
Kotzé, Ds, 82
Kruger, President, 64
Kühnel, Bro., 11
Kuruman, 52f, 73

Lambeth Conference, 69
Langalibalele, 70
Lena, 11
Limpopo River, 60
Lindley, Rev. D., 41f, 73
Livingstone, Dr, 52ff, 74, 88
Livingstone, Mrs, 53
Loedolff, Ds, 82
London Missionary Society, 22, 24, 26f, 32, 34, 38, 40, 52f, 56, 58, 72ff, 85f
Love, Rev. T., 85f
Lovedale, 86ff
Lutherans, 9, 16f
Lydenburg, 61

Mackenzie, Bp, 56f
Macrorie, Bp, 69
Magistrates, 45, 49
Malmesbury, 98
Maoris, 45
Marianhill, 99
Maritz, G., 40
Marriage, 18
Marsveld, Bro., 11
Mashonaland, 77
Matabeles, 41, 52
Matyana, 70

Medical institutions, 45, 88f
Merriman, J. X., 94
Messianism, 90, 104
Methodist Missionary Society, 34, 38
Methodists, 29, 31ff, 37f, 41, 48f, 58, 72ff, 88, 91f, 94, 103
Missionaries, 3, 9, 23, 26f, 30, 34, 36, 38, 41f, 48ff, 52, 54ff, 65f, 72ff, 78, 85, 87ff, 91, 95ff, 101ff
Missionary strategy, 12
Missions, 4, 8, 10, 12, 15, 22, 26, 28, 33, 35, 37, 45ff, 50, 52, 54, 56, 66, 69, 73ff, 81, 86, 89, 96ff, 107
Mobatsa, 53
Moffatt, Mrs, 52
Mokoni, Rev. M., 91f
Moravians, 9ff, 16, 46, 72, 86
Moroka, 74
Moshesh, 43, 74f
Mott, J. R., 103
Mount Coke, 33
Murray, Rev. A. (Snr), 79
Murray, Rev. A. (Jnr), 60, 79ff, 84
Mzilikazi, 41, 52, 58, 73

Namaqualand, 30, 34, 72
Nantes, Edict of, 6
Natal, 1, 40ff, 46, 50, 60f, 65f, 68ff, 73f, 76, 93ff, 99
Native Affairs Commission, 93
Native agents, 12, 86 (*see also* Assistant Missionaries)
Native Laws Amendment Act, 106
Nederduitse Gereformeerde Kerk (*see also* Dutch Reformed Church)
New Testament, 67
New Zealand, 44f
Ngami, Lake, 53
Nguni, 1
Norwegian Missionary Society, 73

Old Testament, 58, 67f
Orange Free State, 43f, 60f, 73f, 80, 93, 100
Orange, Prince of, 13f, 16
Orange River, 38, 43, 60
Orange River Colony (*see* Orange Free State)
Orange River Sovereignty (*see* Orange Free State)
Ordinary, 20
Oxford Movement, 74

Palmerton, 33
Paris Evangelical Missionary Society, 73f, 90
Pass laws, 11, 25
Pentecostalists, 90, 99f
Philip, Fr, 25ff, 37ff, 46, 53
Pietermaritzburg, 39, 42, 58, 67, 99
Political commissioners, 6, 17, 19
Polygamy, 50, 66
Pondoland, 43
Pondos, 49
Port Elizabeth, 24, 31
Portuguese, 2, 54
Postma, Ds D., 63f
Potchefstroom, 59f, 62ff
Potgieter, H., 41, 59
Predikant, 40, 59
Presbyterians, 14, 20f, 52, 79, 85, 94, 103 (*see also* Scotland, Church of)
Presbytery, 14f
Pretoria, 63f
Privy Council, 68, 83

Rationalism, 22, 63, 65, 80
Read, Rev. J., 23, 26f
Reichel, Bp, 10
Republics, 13, 42, 45, 61f, 64, 83, 93
Retief, P., 38f, 42, 60
Rhenish Mission, 72
Rhodesia, 41, 77, 101
Ricards, Bp, 98f
Roman Catholic, 21, 73, 98f, 103
Roodezand, 10
Ross, Rev. J., 86
Royal Geographical Society, 56
Rustenburg, 63f

Sacraments, 3, 10f, 58, 67, 97
St Matthew's, 88
Salem, 33
Sand River Convention, 61
Schmidt, G., 9, 11
Schwinn, Bro., 11
Scotland, 19, 39, 79, 82, 87f
Scotland, Church of, 20, 85
Sechuana, 52
Sects, 90, 92f, 95ff, 102ff
Sekukuni, 76
Sekukuniland, 75, 77, 91
Seminaries, 80, 83, 86, 99, 103
Settlers, 17f, 23, 31, 34, 38, 42, 45
Shaw, Rev. B., 30, 34f, 72f
Shaw, Rev. W., 31ff, 38, 49, 77

Shawbury, 33
Shembe, I., 104
Shepstone, J., 70
Shepstone, Sir T., 46f, 66, 70, 76
Sick-comforter, 3
Slachter's Nek Rebellion, 36
Slaves, 5, 8ff, 15, 25, 37f, 42, 54ff
Sluysken, Governor, 13ff
Smit, E., 40ff
Social gospel, 95
Somerset, Lord C., 11, 30f
South Africa, Union of, 94f
South African General Missionary
  Conference, 101ff
South-West Africa, 1, 72
Soutpansberg, 60f, 64
State-Church, 16f, 63f (*see also*
  Established Church)
Stellenbosch, 8, 10, 83
Stewart, Rev. J., 88, 101
Swaziland, 75, 77
Switzerland, 82
Synods, 17, 19, 39, 61f, 77, 81ff, 95,
  101, 106 (*see also* Assemblies)

Tembus, 91f
Tembu National Church, 90
Temple, Abp, 95
Thaba 'Nchu, 41, 73
Thom, Dr G., 25, 79, 85
Thomas, Rev. J., 48
Thomson, Rev. W., 85
Tile, Rev. N., 91f
Tractarians, 74
Transkei, 2, 91, 96
Transvaal, 55, 59, 61ff, 75ff, 80f, 83,
  91, 93, 95f, 100
Trappists, 98f
Trek, The Great, 36, 39, 59f
Trekkers, 38ff, 55, 58ff, 75
Twells, Bp, 74

United Free Church of Scotland, 96
United Presbyterian Church, 87
Universities' Mission to Central
  Africa, 56

Vaal River, 39, 43, 60, 64
van der Hoff, Ds D., 61ff
Vanderkemp, Dr J. T., 23f, 26f
van der Stel, Governor S., 6
van Lier, Ds H. R., 10
van Riebeeck, Commander J., 2f, 5
Vegkop, Battle of, 41
Volksraad, 42, 58, 62
von Manger, Ds, 15
Vos, Ds M., 10

Watkins, Rev. O., 76ff
Weavind, Rev. G., 76, 78
Wellington, 81
Wesley, Rev. J., 29, 32, 34
Wesleyville, 33
Wilkinson, Bp, 76
Winter, Pastor, 77, 91
Witwatersrand, 78
Witchcraft, 50
Wolseley, Sir G., 69
Women's organizations, 104
Worcester, 80
World Council of Churches, 103
World War II, 95

Xhosas, 2, 48f, 86

Zambesi River, 56, 74, 88
Zinzendorf, Count, 9
Zionists, 90, 96f, 100
Zululand, 56
Zulus, 39, 41ff, 66f, 70f, 73